P9-DXE-845

Opera
Guide

16

Tosca
Puccini

Frontispiece: Maria Callas in the 1964 Covent Garden production by Franco Zeffirelli (photo: Zoe Dominic)

Preface

This series, published under the auspices of English National Opera and The Royal Opera, aims to prepare audiences to enjoy and evaluate opera performances. Each book contains the complete text, set out in the original language together with a current performing translation. The accompanying essays have been commissioned as general introductions to aspects of interest in each work. As many illustrations and musical examples as possible have been included because the sound and spectacle of opera are clearly central to any sympathetic appreciation of it. We hope that, as companions to the opera should be, they are well-informed, witty and attractive.

Nicholas John
Series Editor

16

Tosca

Giacomo Puccini

Opera Guide Series Editor: Nicholas John

Published in association with English National Opera and The Royal Opera

John Calder · London
Riverrun Press · New York

First Published in Great Britain, 1982, by
John Calder (Publishers) Ltd, 18 Brewer Street,
London W1R 4AS

and

First published in U.S.A., 1982 by
Riverrun Press Inc.,
175 Fifth Avenue
New York, NY 10010

BRITISH LIBRARY CATALOGUING IN PUBLICATION DATA
Puccini, Giacomo
    Tosca. — (Opera guide; 16)
    1. Puccini, Giacomo   Tosca
    2. Operas — Librettos
    I. Title   II. John, Nicholas   III. Giacosa, Giuseppe   IV. Illica, Luigi   V. Series
    782.1′092′4   ML.410.P89
    ISBN 0 7145 3772 1

John Calder (Publishers) Ltd, English National Opera and
The Royal Opera House, Covent Garden Ltd receive financial
assistance from the Arts Council of Great Britain. English
National Opera also receives financial assistance from the
Greater London Council.

Typeset in Plantin by Margaret Spooner Typesetting, Dorchester, Dorset.

Printed and bound in Great Britain by Whitstable Litho Ltd., Whitstable, Kent.

Contents

List of Illustrations

Manifest Artifice

Bernard Williams

The criticism of operas, as distinct from the criticism of performances, is still not a very developed activity. In so far as it exists, it has tended to concentrate on discussing the music, rather than operas as dramatic and musical wholes. The fact that there is not much serious criticism of Puccini's operas is not, therefore, necessarily surprising. But such criticism as there is has tended to be hostile or contemptuous, and I suspect that, in this particular case, the lack of serious comment is itself a comment. Puccini is not taken entirely seriously.

At the same time, several of his works are, of course, tirelessly successful with the public, and this is not hard to explain: they are, at their best, immensely and almost indestructibly effective. This fact is sometimes used as a humbling rejoinder to critical doubt — 'so there'. In itself, it is not enough of a rejoinder, but it raises a demand, at least, for more understanding.

We perhaps tend to assume too easily that we understand Puccini, the character of his work, and his place in the history of opera. In fact, he is not easy to place. It is not obvious, for instance, what comparisons it is useful to make with him. If one merely looks around him, to Leoncavallo, or Mascagni, or Giordano, he of course stands out, and his powers of lyrical invention seem magical. If one looks back to Verdi, Puccini becomes a small figure — but then not only was Verdi a great genius, but it was inconceivable that after him anyone could achieve anything of similar scale in Italian opera.

More interestingly, one can look sideways, to Richard Strauss, and indeed there is enough stylistically in common for a certain kind of now rather tired lyricism to be called the 'Puccini–Strauss' style. But they had very different aims and origins. In Italian opera, there was still such a thing as straightforward popular success, and Puccini aimed at it; while Strauss, as a German composer after Wagner, wrote orchestrally complex operas to expressionist or symbolic texts, as well as being a composer of 'serious' music outside the opera house. Strauss was, almost by definition, a more 'serious' composer than Puccini. But it is far from clear that as an opera composer he should therefore be taken more seriously.

Such comparisons in fact effect nothing until one has taken a closer look at what Puccini tried to do, and the individual musico-dramatic methods that he employed. Puccini is no doubt a limited artist, but his limitations, and the failings of his works, are themselves markedly individual. *Tosca* is at the centre of the problem of getting a clear and balanced view of Puccini. Of all his pieces it is one of the most famous for its theatrical effect. It is also distinctly nasty, in a way which helps to bring out critical hostility; in fact, it defines a central form of hostility towards the composer, since the touch of nastiness is typical of him, and *Tosca* presents the best organised example of it. *Butterfly* is also nasty (particularly in the first version, which failed and which has only recently been revived) but it is much more sentimental, and the overall effect is of pathos rather than cruelty. *Turandot* is even more sadistic than *Tosca*—to the extent that, to permit the torture of Liù, the hero's behaviour has to be made barely intelligible — but it is musically more ambitious, and it has the undoubted appeal that it defeated him: for once, Puccini was not so insufferably on top of it all.

7

Tosca is not perfect, even in its own terms, and it is more flawed, perhaps, than *La Bohème*. *Vissi d'arte* is not a very interesting piece which, as Puccini himself later came to feel, holds up the action. In Act Three, Cavaradossi's nostalgic solo before the dénouement, *E lucevan le stelle*, leaves a desultory impression and seems not to contribute enough to the significance of the action. I suspect that in part this is because, like some other Puccini tenor arias — *Nessun dorma* in *Turandot* is an obvious example — it is simply too short, and makes the effect of one shouted sentence rather than any revelation of character.

The words of this aria replaced, at Puccini's insistence, a heroic set of reflections on life and art which, we are told, attracted Verdi's favourable attention when he was shown the libretto. Puccini found that he could do nothing with these, and set instead a reverie on past love-making. That fact in itself is not the cause of the weakness of the scene. Puccini is writing a different kind of work, and in some ways a more modern work, than any to which those heroic reflections would have been appropriate. Cavaradossi, like some other Puccini characters, is a man of softly impressionable sexuality — qualities already clearly expressed at the beginning of the opera in the aria addressed to his painting, *Recondita armonia*. He seems to be a revolutionary hero largely by accident, and his involvement in the action is a good deal more personal than political. Even more striking than *E lucevan* in this direction is his reaction to Tosca's telling him that she has murdered Scarpia: he comes out with the sentimental and very pretty *O dolci mani* which sweetly turns its back on anything that such a murder might mean.

These pieces weaken the Third Act, as his publisher, Giulio Ricordi, indeed complained. They do so not because they are personal and sexual rather than political, but because they do not move anything forward, or contribute any further dimension to what is going to happen. Especially in relation to Puccini's insistence on compressed and rapid action (which he got, presumably, from Verdi), these static moments can seem simply opportunistic — particularly since *O dolci mani* has one of those Puccini melodies that encourage tenors and conductors to reckless amounts of *rubato*.

There are, then, weaknesses in *Tosca*, even in terms of Puccini's own conception of how it should work. But the interesting thing about *Tosca* lies in its suspect strength, in the fact that not only is it operatically successful, but that it is a fundamental example of operatic success. It thus raises a question, not just about Puccini, and the special character of his achievement, but about the nature of opera itself.

There are a few basic ways of being excited and held by the operatic stage. The trio in the last act of *Rosenkavalier* represents one, and *Di quella pira* in *Trovatore* another. *Tosca* at its best displays several. The end of Act One, for instance, with its mounting excitement and its superimposition of a great dark baritone declamation onto the rhythm of a tolling bell and religious ritual, is a splendid example of something that real opera lovers really love. *Tosca*'s continuous success with the public is not a mere triumph of bad taste or a result of contemporary associations, as has been the case with certain works of Meyerbeer, or Gounod, or Menotti. What is compelling in *Tosca* has direct connections with what is compelling in greater operas.

It is hard to think of a parallel to this in non-musical drama. Leaving aside questions of the limitations of his purely musical invention, the critical resistance to Puccini lies principally in the conviction that there is something manipulative or even cynical about his work. That conviction is, in my view, basically right. But that leaves the problem, since these manipulative works resemble, in their capacity to hold us, operas which have no such faults. If

8

Antonio Scotti, the first London and New York Scarpia, who continued to sing the role an exceptional number of times, and Hariclea Darclée, the first Tosca (Stuart-Liff Collection)

opera is at all a serious business, how can this be? This is *the* question about Puccini, and its answer lies in what it is like to experience opera.

W. H. Auden once said* 'in a sense, there can be no tragic opera', because singing itself is too evidently a free and enjoyable activity: 'the singer may be playing the role of a deserted bride who is about to kill herself, but we feel quite certain as we listen that not only we, but also she, is having a wonderful time.'

Auden's remark reminds us that the enjoyment of opera — and it is particularly true of Italian opera — grows tightly round enjoyment of a technique, a *manifest* technique. Here there is an interesting comparison, and an important difference, with conventions of the non-operatic stage. When people who do not care for opera and know nothing about it ridicule the convention of conversation in song, it is right to remind them of other theatrical conventions, in particular the conventions of conversation in blank verse, which they may be less inclined to reject. In watching Shakespeare, one indeed appreciates it as verse — at least, if the director allows one to. Excitement, tension, involvement, are generated by that verse, and by its being verse, but in the opera house, it goes further than this. It is not only song, and the fact that it is song, that generates excitement, but the singer. At a fine operatic performance, we are conscious of the singer's achievement and of the presence of physical style and vitality, and the sense of this reinforces the drama itself. A concrete feeling of performance and of the performers' artistry is nearer the front of the mind than in other dramatic arts. It is because of this that outbreaks of applause (if not these days, the granting of encores) can be appropriate, as they scarcely could be with a play, even one in verse.

Puccini's immense success is connected with the fact that the pleasures of opera, particularly in the Italian style, are in any case involved with an obvious and immediately presented artifice. He was of course ingenious (Toscanini said: 'Puccini is clever, but only clever'), and he was greatly gifted in the creation of theatrical atmospheres and gestures — atmospheres and gestures which *announce themselves* as theatrical. In Act One of *Tosca*, the threatening arrival of Scarpia is synchronised with the climax of the horse-play between the sacristan and the choirboys, in a way which precisely draws attention to

* 'Notes on Music and Opera' in *The Dyer's Hand* (Faber, 1963), pp. 468-9. Auden agreed, however, that opera can be the ideal vehicle of 'tragic myth'. See also 'The World of Opera' in his *Secondary Worlds* (Faber, 1969)

itself as a musical and dramatic device. Similarly, the opening of the Third Act offers a complex and sophisticated texture of bells and a shepherd boy's song which heightens the tension for what is to follow. These effects heighten it in a specially self-conscious and indirect way — by making one conscious all the time that this has been conceived as a preparation for what is to follow.

Again, in the Second Act, Scarpia's arrangement of his treachery gives pleasure through the very theatricality with which it is displayed. His instructions to Spoletta tell him, but not Tosca, that the execution of Cavaradossi is to be only a pretended fake, that the 'simulated' killing is to be a real one. 'As we did in the case of Palmieri', says Scarpia, more than once: 'You understand?' 'Yes' replies Spoletta, as he leaves, 'like Palmieri'. It is appropriate that the subject of this should be a double falsehood, a pretence of a pretence. It is not simply a device of dramatic irony, which puts us into complicity with them against Tosca. It puts us into a complicity with that device itself, with a certain tradition of theatrical effect, and it is in seeing the wheels of artifice turn that we enjoy it.

The idea which Puccini carries further than any other opera composer is that of securing an effect through the audience's consciousness that that is what he is doing. In exploiting this idea, he transfers to the level of musical and dramatic invention something that is always inherent, to some extent, in opera, and the performance of opera; and that is why one can acknowledge the truth of his talent to the nature of opera.

That acknowledged display of artifice, which is Puccini's most characteristic device, is not of course enough to secure his popularity. For that he needed, what he outstandingly had, melodic gifts, orchestral ingenuity, a sense of atmosphere, and a talent for compression. But, granted all that, the peculiarity of his talent does specially define the nature of the popularity that he achieved. In particular, it affects what it is like to see one of his operas with which one is already familiar. With a very great work, to hear it for the twentieth time gives the chance, not just to hear something one has missed, but to understand something new. That is not the point with Puccini, and everybody knows that it is not the point. The aim is, rather, to see him do the trick again; the better one knows the whole thing, and the more familiar the trick, the greater the pleasure, just because the pleasure lies in complicity with his artifice. One enjoys the entry of Scarpia very much more when it is not a surprise — that is to say, when one is not actually surprised by it, but rather knowledgeably looks forward to the effect of the surprise.

It is sometimes held against Puccini's operas that they are melodramatic, but that is certainly not the notable or exceptional thing about them. As the word itself implies, it is hard for operas of strong action to be anything else, and many operatic masterpieces are melodramatic: *Rigoletto*, for instance, or, in good part, *Fidelio*. The special characteristic of Puccini's operas is that they are manipulative — that in place of the direct address of those two works, for instance, or indeed of any work of Verdi's, there is a calculated, and indeed displayed, contrivance to produce a certain emotional effect.

The highly conscious and self-referential character of his method is a very modern feature of Puccini's work, and he could not have stood anywhere but at the end of the tradition of Italian opera, extracting the last drops from it by the method of openly exploiting our consciousness of the ways in which it produced its effects. At the same time, what is achieved through this sensibility is limited — or at any rate defined — by a certain lack of expressive ambition, both musical and dramatic. In his use of swift narration, schematic characters, and deftly indicated moods, together with his self-conscious exploitation of familiar conventions, Puccini is a cinematic artist, and some of

10

Marie Collier in the 1960 Sadler's Wells production, with Peter Glossop as Scarpia (photo: Houston Rogers)

the most natural comparisons that his works invite are with films. Use of a popular melodic style and the conventional directness of his narrative invite comparisons not with 'art' films of, say, German expressionism, but with the finest products of the Hollywood studios in their best days — which indeed, like Puccini, learnt some of their technique from more ambitiously innovative art works. It would be a mistake to take this as an insult to Puccini: these films are so excellent that the comparison gives no reason to underestimate his operas, but merely offers a better perspective from which to enjoy them.

Like many good Hollywood film-makers, moreover, Puccini found it natural to use distant, unreal or fantasy subject matter. In this his operas also resemble, of course, many other operas. But in Puccini's case, something special is effected by the choice of subject. The fact that Verdi's works are remotely placed (with the famous, and at first disastrous, exception of *La Traviata*), and that Wagner's are often placed nowhere at all, imposes in itself no limit at all on their power or honesty or significance. But in Puccini's case, there is something suspect about the exoticism of the oriental pieces, and the fanciful quality of *Bohème*'s Parisian life. They provide an element of distancing, a way in which the work can be exciting or touching without being disturbing. Hollywood constantly used such methods, though it could also — in some of the crime films, for instance — go beyond them.

Here again, *Tosca* is the central and the test case. *Tosca* is, in fact, the exception, the one really twentieth-century subject among Puccini's major works. It is totally unimportant that it is set in Napoleonic times. It really asks to be set in this century, above all in Mussolini's Italy, with Scarpia as a Fascist boss. Many things in the opera fit such a time and such a regime, including the character of the villain. Scarpia's corruption, and the sense, which I have already mentioned, that Cavaradossi is a man with other interests who got into it all by accident, conspire to make the torture scene more a psycho-sexual event than anything political, and this is a recognisably modern motif, of a kind inconceivable, certainly, in Verdi.

Yet it is just here, where Puccini gets close to a disturbing reality, that his method of exploiting the traditions of Italian opera rather than transforming them ceases to work, and the displayed artifice stops being any longer an acceptable source of pleasure. He was very skilful, for the most part, in avoiding that situation, by taking an exotic or fanciful subject matter, or very schematically indicated situations of horror or pathos. (It is ironical that *verismo* should be the name given to some of these devices.) A danger always lay for him in the real strength of his fascination with violence, what he himself called his 'Neronic instinct'. In some cases, notably *La Fanciulla del West*, he channelled it in a direction of schematic fantasy which leaves room for his devices to work. In at least one case — parts of *Turandot* —the obsession rises above the devices.

In the Second Act of *Tosca*, however, his sadistic imagination pulls too strongly on what is indeed one of his most carefully structured pieces of artifice. The effect is one that many have found disturbing and disagreeable, and much more so than some other operas which contain, in terms of their action, equally brutal material. The careful placing of Cavaradossi's off-stage cries, gets its effect, like the earlier use of Tosca's off-stage concert, once more through the consciousness of artifice: the music invites us to hear the effect being created. But the tension has been sufficiently raised, Scarpia is enough of a figure, the subject is close enough to reality, for pleasure not to run easily through such craftily constructed channels. Puccini's best effects come about through the manifest *use* of feeling, of circumstance, and of the audience; police torture, if we get near enough to an adequate representation of it, cannot be used in this way.

That there should be something nasty at the centre of *Tosca* is the result of Puccini's method when it goes beyond the bounds of what it can handle. The method is a special and very effective invention, and it has a powerful appeal which is rooted in the traditions of Italian opera, and indeed in the basic experience of its performance. But the method cannot deal with a genuinely threatening content, and when it fails, the spectator's revulsion is considerable, for he feels himself not only exploited, but an accomplice in his own exploitation. *Tosca* is remarkable in providing some of the most striking achievements of Puccini's artifice, and also the most unnerving display of its limitations.

The music of Puccini's 'Tosca'

Bernard Keeffe

In 1924 Cecil Gray wrote: 'No living composer is more despised and execrated by the leaders of musical opinion in every country than Puccini'. Some thirty years later, an American professor* dismissed *Tosca* as a 'shabby little shocker'. Cecil Gray was a composer as well as a writer, and it is perhaps cruel to mention that his operas are unperformed and forgotten. The academic may find in *Tosca* little evidence of macrotonality, but even he surely must admit that for more than eighty years Puccini's operas have filled the seats of the world's theatres and erased the red ink in many a balance sheet. Continuing success may not be everything, but like money, it does help, and might persuade us that Puccini was after all a genius.

I believe that within its terms of reference *Tosca* is a masterpiece. It is a shocker, certainly, but much more, and there is no doubt that its impact derives from the music. If you doubt this, ask yourself why the play upon which it is based has long ago disappeared from the stage, and name an opera which has survived on the strength of the story alone. Even Cecil Gray had to confess that in the theatre Puccini's magic worked, and it is in the theatre, not in the study, that his music must be judged.

Puccini once said that God touched him with his little finger and said 'Write only for the theatre'. He willingly obeyed, and added that he could compose only when he could see his creations before his mind's eye moving, gesturing and singing 'in the great window of the stage'. He often composed at night, and in the silence of his darkened room used to laugh at their joys and their passionate love affairs, then condemn them to death and weep, literally weep, at their dying phrases. For this he needed characters and situations into which he could pour his archetypal musical expression, which acted directly on the emotions of his audience.

The play *La Tosca* by the French dramatist Sardou offered just such a subject, and Puccini had cast longing eyes at it for several years. He was not alone; Verdi admired it, and had said that if he had been younger he would gladly have set it to music. Franchetti, a minor contemporary of Puccini's, even went so far as to get Sardou's consent to his commissioning a treatment from Luigi Illica, one of Puccini's librettists for *Manon Lescaut* and *La Bohème*. Illica mentioned this to Puccini, and was prompted to persuade Franchetti, with surprisingly little difficulty, to give up his plans. This was the third time that Puccini had thumbed his nose at a rival and the fourth time that he had gone to French literature for his subject. *Edgar* (1889) had been based on a play by Alfred de Musset, *Manon Lescaut* (1893) on the novel by Prévost, already set by Massenet, while *La Bohème* (1896) derived from a book by Murger, also made into an opera by Leoncavallo. There are several reasons for the appeal that French subjects had for Puccini, and not least was the music of Massenet, whose operas enjoyed great success in Italy and strongly influenced the development of the style characterised as *verismo*. While this cannot be exactly identified with the realism of French novels and plays such as those of Zola and Sardou, it shares with them the aim of presenting aspects

---

* Joseph Kerman *Opera as Drama*, 1956.

Mariano Stabile as Scarpia at La Scala.
He sang the role at Covent Garden in the
1920s (Royal Opera House Archives)

Lina Cavalieri as Tosca in the early part of
the century (Royal Opera House Archives)

of life which bourgeois society preferred to hide. Massenet fumigated his stories for his fashionable audience, but developed a vivid emotionalism which was a model for Puccini's less inhibited muse.

Victorien Sardou was the prince of the Parisian theatre, and the master of the well-made play, a vain and irrepressible man who ruthlessly manipulated his actors as well as his audience in his search for success. He had constructed *La Tosca* as a vehicle for Sarah Bernhardt in 1887 and provided her with a sensational triumph, and his pocket with a flood of royalties. The play was set in Rome in June 1800 at the time of Napoleon's victory at Marengo; it is a story of revolution, repression, police corruption, torture, murder and rape. Melodrama? Perhaps, but the first night of *Tosca* was almost ruined by the threat of a terrorist bomb, and real life was not so different then as now. But is this the stuff of art? Certainly, for this story shows the strength of the human spirit, as two innocent people, trapped in the eddies of the whirlpool of politics, sacrifice their lives out of loyalty and love.

But now Sardou's play had to be turned into an opera. At first even Puccini had doubts about his suitability, and expressed them openly to Sardou: '.... and the more I said that it should be composed by a Frenchman, the more he insisted that it needed an Italian hand, that it should be a Roman opera. When I pleaded that my style was too gentle, too delicate, and that my music moved on a different plane of expression, he retorted that there was no such thing, only talent. I pointed out that my heroines, Manon and Mimi, were different types from his, and then he shouted: "Tosca is their sister to the life—women in love are all the same!", and I had to admit defeat'. No doubt Sardou had his eye on his very substantial royalty and knew that if anyone could make a successful opera out of his play it would be Puccini.

The composer now turned to his masterly collaborators, Illica and Giacosa, one to provide the scenario, the other the poetry. Illica had already made a start with the outline he had prepared for Franchetti, but Giacosa as usual grumbled, and worked only under protest. Their task was to reduce Sardou's

Otakar Kraus as Scarpia at Covent Garden in 1953 (Royal Opera House Archives)

five acts to three, and to replace his wordy dialogue with the poetic shorthand upon which Puccini could work his magic. They were so successful that Sardou himself admitted later that their libretto was superior in construction to his play, although they scrapped many of his scenes and characters, and transferred incidents from one location to another. The only character whose departure I regret was the composer Paisiello, whom Sardou depicted as an opportunist lickspittle, as ready to pen a revolutionary hymn as a royalist *Te Deum*. He is flattened by Tosca in her best prima donna manner in an amusing scene where they make ready to perform his new cantata. There is one other choice detail in the play which English audiences would have relished: Angelotti was originally jailed because he recognised in Emma Hamilton, the wife of the British Ambassador to Naples and the Queen's intimate friend, the faded beauty of a teenage whore he once picked up in Vauxhall Gardens!

As always Puccini played a dominating role in the process of dramatic construction, and bullied his librettists unceasingly; he suggested the shape of scenes, dictated the length of lines and even told them where to put the stresses. To demonstrate the sound of the words he wanted, he made up doggerel verses. Although he was dealing with figures as distinguished in their time (and as different in their literary styles) as John Osborne or Christopher Fry today, he had no hesitation in telling them how to do their job, because it was an integral part of his own. What he desired above all was a natural text, simple and brief, in a flowing conversational style; yet it had to be poetry and was often in rhyme. He had no time for pretension and pomposity, for he wanted his characters to respond spontaneously like real men and women. A particularly revealing example of this is Cavaradossi's aria in the last act just before he expects to be executed. Puccini scrapped the original draft, a high-flown farewell to life and art which had mightily impressed Verdi, and insisted on replacing it with what he asserted was the more natural response of an artist facing imminent death. At a session with his collaborators, he played through the rough shape of the melody with improvised words.

Two pre-First World War Toscas: left, Geraldine Farrar; right, Aino Ackté (Stuart-Liff Collection)

Almost shyly he expounded his conception: Cavaradossi would remember his beloved through each of the senses, the sight of the stars, the perfume of the night air, the sound of her step. After the place, the person: *'Entrava ella fragrante'* — the intoxicating scent of a marvellous creature. She falls into his arms, and as he relives embraces and kisses, trembling he uncovers her body, and remembers the touch of her skin. But the dream of love is over now for ever . . . and (literally) 'I die despairing': (*'Muoio disperato'*). Puccini insisted on these words from the start, and Giacosa willingly incorporated them into his delicate poetry.

Puccini had a fanatical obsession with atmosphere and authenticity. He consulted a priest friend about the correct prayers for a service of thanksgiving; he needed to know the exact sound of the church bells of Rome at dawn, even to the precise pitch of the great bell of St Peter's, *er campanone* — it was E natural. He consulted an expert for a genuine folk-song of the Campagna for the shepherd-boy. Above all he knew that he must compose music which would convey the utmost dramatic intensity; he had to grasp the audience's attention from the start and not let go until the fall of the curtain brought them back to everyday life. Sardou might take many minutes of dialogue to set up a situation and describe the characters, but for Puccini the fine print of Cavaradossi's flirtation with French revolutionary ideas was irrelevant. One of the few clumsy lines in the opera is an untypical verbal signpost when Cavaradossi greets *'Angelotti! Il Console della spenta repubblica romana'* (which used to be translated as 'the Consul of the moribund Roman republic'!) often at such a gabble that the phrase and its significance evade the most attentive ear. Sardou's characters are curiously lifeless in the play, despite elaborate dialogue; Puccini's throb with passion, and immediately demand our attention. The secret is in the characterisation through leading themes. Add to this his harmonic sensibility, his genius for orchestral expression, and a sense of drama that fascinates the most reluctant spectator, and you have an array of skills that explains his undiminished appeal.

Medea Mei-Figner as Tosca and the Sicilian baritone Mario Sammarco, a 'sinister and impressive Scarpia' (Stuart-Liff Collection)

Puccini's use of symbolic motifs owes more to the example of Massenet than Wagner. They are not so much visiting cards as triggers of conditioned reflexes; whatever form they take, however fragmentary, they evoke that twitch of emotion that keeps us on the edge of the seat. Take the opening bars, where a sequence of three chords tells us more in six seconds about a man of violence than six minutes of discussion of his motives and character [1]. These chords are not just violent; they are harmonically unrelated, and so symbolise the irrational acts of a psychopath, the sadistic Chief of Police, Baron Scarpia. It is a most potent musical image that recurs throughout the opera, in many different moods, according to the tempo, loudness, register, and orchestration. So when the escaped prisoner, Angelotti, finds the key to the chapel where he can hide, the Scarpia theme is momentarily defeated as its third chord drops suddenly to *pianissimo*. And in the exquisite opening to the last act, the peace of a summer night is clouded by the intrusion of those menacing harmonies: even after his death, Scarpia's evil still threatens.

While it would be too much to claim that Puccini was a cerebral composer of the order of Schönberg, he was a supreme musical craftsman, and part of his strength lay in his manipulation of these symbolic themes in a subtle and often complex relationship. If, for example, you take the top notes of the Scarpia sequence of chords, it forms a chromatic upward phrase. Reverse this, expand is a little, and you have the theme which expresses the other side of his personality as shown at the start of the Second Act, where in an expansive mood he sits at the supper table [20]. But this three note figure can take on a sudden menace during the interrogation, achieving the maximum effect with the simplest means, which might almost be taken as Puccini's motto. There are many other examples of this interrelation of themes. At the very beginning of the opera, after the audience has been gripped by the thunder of the first three bars, the curtain rises on the interior of a church, and the ragged figure of a man runs in to the sound of a hectic sequence of syncopated chords, forming a downward scale of four notes [2]. Angelotti, the escaped political prisoner, is

searching for the key to the chapel where he can hide, left by his sister, the Countess Attavanti. She has been visiting the church, ostensibly to pray, but unwittingly has also acted as model for Cavaradossi's picture of the Magdalen. She too has her musical symbol, and since she was born an Angelotti, what else would it be but a downward scale of four notes? [6] Cavaradossi, in the famous aria *'Recondita armonia'* (literally — 'Strange harmony of contrasts' [8]) speaks of his achievement in combining the looks of his dark-eyed beloved, Tosca, with those of his fair-haired blue-eyed model, who unknown to him is the Countess Attavanti. One commentator has sneered at the lack of 'strange harmony' here, but he has missed the point that in the fifth and sixth bars [9] Puccini has combined, or harmonised, the musical symbol for Tosca, a series of downward dropping intervals [7] with the four note scale [6] associated with the Countess Attavanti. There is also a consistent contour to the music that expresses Cavaradossi's emotions; this often begins with a warm upward scale [15]. Clearly Puccini also associates the rhythm of those triplets with an embrace, although it may be warm, as in the lovers' music, or perverse as in Scarpia's lust [19, 20]. Similarly the chromatic scale always pervades thoughts of jealousy [11]. Sometimes Puccini changes the mood of a phrase by a subtle transformation of its rhythm or tonality; for example, the sinister march of the interrogation squad reappears in the Third Act as the lilting theme which accompanies the lovers' thoughts of freedom [23].

A more complex development is that of the upward-thrusting *arpeggio* which expresses Scarpia's lust [29]. In the last act Tosca describes how she stabbed Scarpia as he tried to rape her, and now the upward *arpeggio* symbolises the thrust of the knife culminating in a splendid top C. Cavaradossi, astonished that her gentle hands could perform such an act, takes them and kisses them, and now the upward *arpeggio* is softened into a melodic caress [37]. This passage was not to the liking of Ricordi, who urged Puccini to replace it with something grander; he missed the point that the composer wanted to express the tender feelings of a real human being, who

18

would speak and act in just such an intimate manner. Another remarkable quality of Puccini's themes is that they can bear many modes of expression. The melody of Cavaradossi's Third Act aria is heard in the warm sound of the strings, in the plaintive hesitant tone of the clarinet, in the passionate sound of the voice, doubled by the full orchestra, and in the closing bars of the opera is thundered out in tragic defiance. The accepted interpretation of this melody uses an extensive *rubato*, not written but enshrined in a tradition based on the composer's instruction.

Puccini's melodies, particularly the arias, look surprisingly simple: there are few chromatic notes, and they often revolve round one note in a manner which looks as though it would sound monotonous but does not. Their harmonies are often just as straightforward. Puccini's harmonic imagination is more evident in his creation of dramatic atmosphere and changes of mood by sudden shifts of tonality and the juxtaposition of apparently unrelated chords. The opening bars [1] are a good example. So too is the music that accompanies Angelotti's first entrance [2]: a series of diminished fifths in ever changing rhythm which seem to be searching for a key, just like the fugitive. When Tosca is telling her lover about her plans for the evening, she sings in one key, while he, preoccupied with thoughts about Angelotti, answers in another. The shifts of tonality can carry the listener along with unrelenting power, as in the love scene in the First Act, where Cavaradossi reassures the jealous Tosca and sweeps into the key of E flat with a phrase like a caress [15]. Often the change of harmony is abrupt and devastating. As Scarpia gives orders to the torturer, he tells him to follow the usual procedure, and adds '. . . later . . . I'll instruct you . . . !', and with these words, across the tonality of E minor comes a chord of G minor, played with chilling effect by the whole orchestra *pianissimo*. (I must confess, however, that I wish Puccini had avoided that banal chord of the dominant seventh just before the last bar of the First Act.)

Placido Domingo as Cavaradossi and Gwyneth Jones as Tosca at Covent Garden in 1971 (photo: Donald Southern)

Roderick Jones and Victoria Sladen in the 1946 Sadler's Wells production (photo: Angus McBean)

To return to more telling procedures, let me quote a passage which recurs several times, apparently whenever the idea of escape, disappearance or concealment is mentioned. This is heard first when Cavaradossi mentions the well in his garden where Angelotti could hide; from the orchestra comes a series of chords built on the whole-tone scale, with shifting nebulous harmonies as though the tonality were dissolving. This sequence is heard again in the Second Act, when Tosca breaks down before Scarpia's coercion and reveals where Angelotti is concealed, and again when Scarpia instructs Spoletta in the trick execution which is supposed to allow the lovers to escape.

This harmonic subtlety is often coloured by Puccini's genius for the orchestra. Every composer evolves a style suited to his needs, and we can admire the delicacy of Mozart or Debussy, as well as the opulence of Richard Strauss or Wagner. Puccini is concerned with the expressive power of the voice, and his accompaniments are invariably transparent or supportive. There is no reason why you should not be able to hear every word in a performance of his operas. He knows where the voice is weak, and where strong, and will thicken the instrumentation when the singer is in the penetrating upper register, but refine it to almost nothing with a passage in the middle or low _parlando_ range, using _pizzicato_ notes or chords and phrases for the woodwind and harp. He is often accused of doubling the voice part with an excess of instrumental tone; he certainly does this occasionally, but it is in the Italian tradition, and I wonder why Verdi is not taxed with this sin in the _Agnus Dei_ of the _Requiem_? This colouring of the melody is in a sense its harmonisation. It was also Puccini's practice to give the voice a sort of monotone, with the main theme in the orchestra, as in both the tenor arias and in part of _'Vissi d'arte'_. At such moments his delicate handling of instrumental colour is easily ignored or taken for granted. For example, the theme that seems to express Tosca's inner piety tells us more about her true character than the long recital of her early history in the play. The deep impression that this makes is due largely to the scoring for flute and cello solo, accompanied by _pizzicato_ triplets for violins and violas [13].

Considering his genius for orchestral colour it is always a surprise to find virtually no examples of his music in the standard books on orchestration. I

Claudio Muzio as Tosca (On May 16, 1905 she replaced the indisposed Edvina as Tosca at Covent Garden, singing opposite Caruso, and gave a performance that was 'thoroughly and fervently Italian in every detail both of voice and infinite variety of gesture, and it was truly wonderful'.)

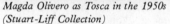

Magda Olivero as Tosca in the 1950s
(Stuart-Liff Collection)

Jean Nadolavitch and Emmy
Destinn (Stuart-Liff Collection)

know of few composers who understood so well the emotional potential of every instrument in the orchestra. Richard Strauss boasted that he could describe any object with his music; Puccini might have claimed that he could trigger any emotion with just the sound of an instrument in a certain register, or in a particular lay-out of a chord. The most obvious example of this is in the brutal rasp of the heavy brass in the opening bars, but contrast that with the sinister sound of three flutes in unison in a low register playing the sinister march of the torture squad [23], or the plangent moan of the viola, either solo or tutti, which dominates so much of this opera. The horrifying atmosphere of the closing bars of the Second Act, when Tosca places candles beside the body of Scarpia, derives almost entirely from the scoring of the chord of E minor in several different combinations, culminating in a sort of shriek with the cor anglais and the violas at the top, muted horns and oboes in the middle, and the distant threat of the executioners' drum. Right at the end of the act the key shifts suddenly back to F sharp minor, but by a touch of genius the final chord played by the harp, celesta and trumpets, lacks the fifth — a bare minor third, F sharp and A. The origin of this is to be found in Scarpia's menacing question to Tosca: '*Ebbene?*' sung to a phrase of a minor third. She bitterly inclines her head, and in the following bars that interval keeps sounding in the orchestra like a nagging pain, and when she picks up the knife and stabs him, that interval of the minor third rings out again and again in the wild fury of Scarpia's dying convulsions.

In utter contrast to these orchestral shudders, the opening of the Third Act is a masterpiece of aural scene painting. It starts with the exuberant open-air sound of four horns in unison, playing the exultant theme that the lovers are later to sing in triumph, as they think, over evil [39]. As their tone dies away the curtain rises; according to the stage directions it is still night, and Puccini's glittering orchestration evokes the starry magic of the last moments before the sunrise. Stealthily the dawn reveals the sinister battlements of the Castel Sant'Angelo, which to the Italians had something of the menace that the Tower of London once had for the English, a charnel house of torture and execution. There is a passing hint of menace in an echo of Scarpia's music, and then a shepherd-boy is heard singing a folksong of the Campagna, with the bells of his flock adding a delicate accompaniment. Puccini was fascinated by the sound of bells, and at this point he creates an unforgettable tonal picture, as the strings of the orchestra unfold a long and wistful melody to the sound of the churchbells of Rome. He took great trouble to get their pitch, rhythm and location absolutely correct so that they could be placed at the right spot backstage and sound louder or more distant as the case might be. Some of them had to be specially made, and to this day it is a passage which can stretch a theatre's resources. In fact no audience in Britain has ever heard the E natural of *er campanone*, which is usually replaced by one an octave higher doubled by a large gong. (You can hear the true pitch in the famous recording conducted by De Sabata at La Scala, Milan.)

The hypnotic beauty of the opening of this act is part of a carefully calculated dramatic sequence, typical of Puccini's mastery of the theatre. Each mood prepares the way for the next: after the vigorous optimism of the opening, we are lulled by the beauty of the night; then comes a hint of menace, dispelled by the innocent charm of the shepherd-boy. As the bells sound, the strings touch deeper wells of melancholy, until with the sombre stroke of the bell of St Peter's, the orchestra unfolds the plaintive melody of Cavaradossi's aria, in which he remembers with growing despair the sensuous joy of a night of love. As the last notes of the aria die away, the orchestra picks up the phrase and reveals that it is the start of the Tosca motif [7] and in a thrilling outburst of orchestral polyphony, and a breathtaking sequence of modulations, the lovers are reunited. This dramatic continuity, heightened by contrast and intensified by changes of key and instrumental colour, typifies Puccini's method throughout the opera. Each entrance is prepared musically to increase the dramatic impact; Scarpia's entrance in the First Act, for example, terrifies the more because it abruptly cuts across the jaunty merrymaking of the Sacristan and his choirboys. Tosca is heard off-stage before she appears, so heightening our expectation. The sound of her voice in the pastiche cantata in the Second Act emphasises the grisly horrors being enacted in Scarpia's rooms. Although the torture sequence is often scorned for its crude sensationalism, its impact is almost wholly created by the music. Puccini shrewdly keeps the actual torture off-stage, and with a meticulously planned *crescendo* of rhythm and dynamics screws up our imagination as tightly as Tosca's nerves. Only in one place does one feel that Puccini yielded to the empty conventions of Italian opera: in Scarpia's aria at the beginning of the Second Act. It is as though he felt bound to give the leading baritone his moment of glory [22] but this attempt at a *Credo* has an empty ring, and we can sense the relief with which Puccini returns to the dramatic action. Cavaradossi's revolutionary outburst at the news of Napoleon's victory is hysterical, but then it would be, wouldn't it? This is one moment when Sardou knew better; in the play the dispatch from the battlefield is read out loud by the Princess at a grand party. As the facts emerge her voice falters and she faints. We could hardly expect that from Scarpia!

Puccini knew what he was doing to discard these subsidiary characters and the verbal intricacies that might have entertained Sardou's Parisian audience; they had no place in his operatic method. What he needed was a taut dramatic structure where his musical genius could present the characters as archetypal figures and his success in doing so accounts for his universal appeal.

Nearly sixty years ago Cecil Gray could attack Puccini and claim the support of 'the leaders of musical opinion in every country'. In 1982 Sir William Walton remarked that 'Puccini is almost my favourite composer' and selected as one of his 'Desert Island Discs', Cavaradossi's aria *'E lucevan le stelle'*.

Linda Esther Gray as Tosca in 1981 at ENO (photo: Andrew March)

Scarpia's first entrance at La Scala in 1959 (Teatro alla Scala)

Maria Callas and Tito Gobbi in Act Two in the 1964 Covent Garden production

Historical Perspectives on 'Tosca'

Stuart Woolf

Giacomo Puccini was a babe-in-arms when Italy was united in 1861. So the final scenes of the prolonged epic drama of the Italian struggle for independence and unification which had enthused the European public — the invasion of Sicily and Naples by Garibaldi and his Thousand — can hardly have formed part of his childhood impressions. But as a boy of thirteen he must have been affected by the national rejoicing in September 1870, when the walls of the Eternal City were breached and Rome became the capital of Italy. *Tosca* was written only in the late 1890s. But Puccini's youthful experiences as an Italian cannot be ignored as they surely influenced his understanding and interpretation of major events in Italy's historical past. Puccini belonged to the first generation of a new nation-state which (like most new states) was concerned to legitimate its existence by a self-laudatory interpretation of the inevitability of its creation. At school the young Giacomo was no doubt taught this 'official' version of the *Risorgimento,* a rapidly invented and uniformly recounted tale, in which martyrs and heroes, sometimes squabbling but always united in their patriotism, served as the milestones in the victorious march towards monarchical unity. Inevitably, in so simplistically mythologised a story, the rulers of those Italian states who had opposed the house of Savoy were castigated, usually for their maladministration as much as for their reactionary views.

Thus, for Puccini, the major political events which form the background to *Tosca* were part of his education as an Italian, before he ever saw Sardou's play. The Bourbons of Naples and the Popes of Rome were opponents of the Italian patriots in 1799-1800, as in 1848 or 1859-61. Indeed, for Puccini (and perhaps for Sardou?) Atto Vannucci's *Martyrs of Italian Liberty from 1794 to 1848* (republished for the seventh time in 1887) may well have provided the primary source of inspiration for the portrayal of the consul Cesare Angelotti, patriot of the Roman republic. This minor character, almost the archetypal persecuted patriot in both Sardou's drama and Puccini's opera, was based on the historically less pure figure of Liborio Angelucci, a consul of the Roman republic whose speculation in confiscated ecclesiastical properties and lust for power led to his enforced resignation; far from being assassinated by the Neapolitan or any other police, Angelucci died in his bed in 1811.

To Puccini and his public, the events of 1799-1800 were more distant and unfocussed than is the Victorian era to most British opera-goers today. But that these events should have been reduced simply to early names in the rollcall of patriotic martyrdom is not entirely casual. For, to the monarchical historians of the end of the nineteenth century, the legacy of this first political expression of national sentiment was uncomfortably ambivalent. Political consciousness among small groups of educated Italians — nobles, reformers, writers, even priests — had been aroused by the first French invasion of Italy under the young general Napoleon Bonaparte in 1796. The Italian collaborators of the invading French armies were described by their enemies, somewhat unjustly, as 'jacobins'. In fact, their moment of glory only came some years after Robespierre and his fellow jacobins had been guillotined in France. During these three years of French rule (1796-99), the Italian patriots

25

discussed and publicly proclaimed their beliefs, which can be summarised as faith in independence, some form of unity, a close relationship with France, democracy and a republic. The established rulers of Italy were evicted, with Charles Emanuel IV of Savoy, King of Sardinia, followed by the Austrian ruler of Lombardy, Emperor Francis II, his client dukes of Modena, Parma and Tuscany, and Pope Pius VI and Ferdinand IV of Naples. Republics were created on the model of France — the Cisalpine and Ligurian republics in northern Italy (1797), the Roman republic (February 1798) and the Parthenopean at Naples (January 1799).

The patriots who played a role in these republics were imbued with idealistic faith in the possibilities of change and progress; revolution was to succeed where the enlightened reforms of the previous decades had failed. This continuity between enlightened reform and revolution was an established canon of eighteenth century historiography. Sardou, concerned as always to validate his historical realism, gave Cavaradossi impeccable credentials: his father, a friend of Galiani, Diderot and d'Alembert, married a relative of Helvétius, while Mario himself learnt his art from the revolutionary painter David. In the opera, the same identification of enlightened rationalistic philosophy with revolutionary beliefs is pithily conveyed in Scarpia's aside that Cavaradossi 'believes in Voltaire!'

But the exactions of the French troops and the failure of the Italian jacobins to win over the peasantry by an attack on feudal rights (as in France in 1789) led to savage risings against both French and patriots as the Allied coalition under the Russian general Suvorov defeated the French armies in the spring of 1799. In the kingdom of Naples a peasant army led by cardinal Ruffo in the name of the *Santa Fede* ('Holy Faith') marched up through Calabria and Basilicata, and finally, with the aid of the urban plebs, the *lazzaroni*, captured the city of Naples from the republicans in June. Similar to this Sanfedist peasant reaction, with its superstitiously religious overtones, was the Arezzo peasant rising — to the cry of *Viva Maria* — that accompanied the French withdrawal from Tuscany. At Rome the popolino, or poor, of Trastevere attacked the recently emancipated Jews in the names of the Virgin and the Pope. By August 1799 the French ambassador, Bertolio, could write to Paris: 'We're stranded at Rome as on Robinson Crusoe's island; but our position is far more worrying'. By the end of September, as the French armies withdrew from Italy, only leaving garrisons to defend the ports of Genoa and Ancona, the Italian republics collapsed.

This first episode of the awakening of an Italian national consciousness was thus complex and ambivalent for later generations to interpret. Small groups of educated Italians had proclaimed, and endeavoured to act upon, their belief in independence and some form of unity. But they had proved entirely dependent on the foreign French, and in any case were identified with revolutionary republicanism and jacobin extremism. Their opponents lent themselves to similarly alternative interpretations. For did not the mass risings of the peasantry and urban plebs, although often as much class-based as religiously-inspired, represent a more authentic national voice of Italy than the Italian jacobins? But it was a voice of reaction, in support of a retrograde monarchy and a superstitious faith in priests. To the historians of the monarchical state of Italy, recently unified at the expense of the King of Naples and the Pope, it was easier to ignore such embarrassing problems by concentrating on the fate of the martyrs.

Ferdinand of Naples offered them the perfect excuse. Following the occupation of Naples, Cardinal Ruffo had offered honourable terms to the Neapolitan patriots and French who still held out in the city's two great castles. The British fleet, under Horatio Nelson and carrying the ambassador Sir William Hamilton and his wife Emma, reached Naples the day after the agreement was signed. Whatever the influence of his lover Emma Hamilton, confidante of the violently anti-jacobin queen Maria Carolina, Nelson reneged on the capitulation agreement, hung one of its leaders, Francesco Caracciolo (who was discovered in hiding half way down a well), and held all the others prisoner until Ferdinand could return from Sicily and execute them. This massacre of over a hundred republicans created immediate revulsion and has permanently blackened the reputation of the Bourbons. For it was not only the number of those executed that horrified contemporaries, but their quality, including many of the most distinguished Neapolitan nobles and intellectuals. The patriotic movement in the kingdom of Naples was only to revive a generation later, in the Carboneria and other anti-Bourbon sects which rose in revolt in 1820 and 1848.

In his *The Bourbons of Naples (1734-1825)* (1956) Harold Acton, descendant of an Irish admiral and leading minister of Ferdinand IV, as well as of the liberal Catholic historian Lord Acton, is almost alone among historians over the past century in his attempt to justify Bourbonic rule. For the repressions and breaking of faith following the collapse of the 1820 and 1848 revolutions merely served to confirm the reputation acquired by the Bourbon dynasty in 1799. Gladstone's denunciation of Bourbonic police and prisons, in his *Two Letters to the Earl of Aberdeen on the State Prosecutions of the Neapolitan Government*, was so spectacularly successful (with at least nine reprints in 1851, its year of publication) not least because it built upon a sadly-established reputation. Whether the police were so effective in Scarpia's time is a different matter, and must be regarded as extremely unlikely. Systematic use of secret police as a major instrument of state control only really began in Habsburg Austria in the 1790s and Napoleonic France a decade later. But, given the historical tradition, it is hardly surprising that Sardou and Puccini should have attributed such efficacy to the servants of this ill-starred dynasty.

After so lengthy a digression, it is time to turn back to the events of 1799-1800. The Neapolitan army, under the Austrian general Mack, had already

Joseph Schwarz as Scarpia at Covent Garden in 1925 (Royal Opera House Archives)

Ljuba Welitsch as Tosca in the early 1950s at Covent Garden (Royal Opera House Archives)

occupied Rome in December 1798, when the French had withdrawn for tactical reasons. During these few weeks, before Mack was defeated by the French in a series of battles, Ferdinand of Naples and Maria Carolina had lodged in their Neapolitan embassy at Rome, Palazzo Farnese, where Act Two of *Tosca* takes place. On September 27, 1799, after the French withdrawal, a rabble army advancing from Naples again occupied Rome. It is during this second occupation that the entire action of *Tosca* takes place. Two points of historical interest are worthy of note. First, the atmosphere of fear and menace in the opera rings true. For, although Ferdinand refused to leave Palermo for Rome, the inhabitants of the papal capital must have felt peculiarly vulnerable, as their city was transferred from one foreign occupant to another. Indeed the death in exile of Pius VI in August 1799 left the Romans without a legal temporal ruler until the election of Pius VII in 1800.

Secondly, the close interlocking between Tosca's personal love-affair with Cavaradossi and the sudden change of course marked by the battle of Marengo, although obviously accentuated by Sardou and Puccini for melodramatic effect, reflects a moment of genuine historical significance. (Perhaps Italian history contains more than its fair share of such dramatic episodes, from the rivalry of clans in medieval Verona which inspired Shakespeare's *Romeo and Juliet*, to Garibaldi and indeed more recent episodes. Or maybe the very continuity of Italian cultural hegemony in Europe, from the twelfth to the seventeenth century, imprinted a heightened and over-dramatised sense of Italian history on European writers and poets.) In one respect Sardou and Puccini distort the historical record. For Bourbon complacency about the defeat of revolutionary France had little basis. The day before the second Neapolitan occupation of Rome, Suvorov had been defeated at the battle of Zurich and forced to withdraw his army into Germany; soon after the Tsar abandoned his coalition. Thus the continuance of Bourbon power rested solely on Austrian military skill. Only five weeks later, soon after his return from Egypt, Napoleon Bonaparte seized power on the 18th Brumaire (November 9 1799). While Napoleon assured himself of France, the Austrian armies under Mélas took the offensive in Liguria, capturing Nice on May 11 and finally gaining Genoa on June 4. But Napoleon had already crossed the Great Saint Bernard pass across the Alps in mid-May, and on June 14 1800, dramatically reversing what initially had seemed a defeat, won his decisive victory at Marengo. Within weeks the Cisalpine and Ligurian republics were re-established and Piedmont placed under French military rule; the Neapolitans hastily withdrew from Rome, which the new pope Pius VII entered in early July. All Italy was to remain firmly under Napoleonic control, with the Bourbons of Naples deposed in 1806 (but surviving under British naval protection in Sicily), and Rome occupied in 1808; only with Napoleon's overthrow in 1814 were king and pope to be restored to their thrones.

Marengo was thus a battle of true historical importance: it consolidated Napoleon's power in France and enabled him to renew his victorious campaigns in his ever more aggressive quest for the military domination of Europe. But Marengo also and immediately was transmuted into more than its historical reality. Its iconographical representation, reproduced and diffused in innumerable versions, made of the event a symbol of Napoleon the Great, conqueror and liberator, in the grand classical and neo-classical tradition that looked back unashamedly to Alexander. To the Italians, in the late 1890s, this image probably only survived in opaque and tarnished form, for official Italian historiography — in those decades of bitter rivalry between France and Italy — preferred to forget about the Napoleonic years and date

Act Two in the 1959 production at La Scala (Teatro alla Scala)

the beginning of the *Risorgimento* to 1815. But for Sardou the Napoleon of Marengo undoubtedly constituted an indelible fragment of his culture.

One final aspect of *Tosca* must be noted — its persistent tone of anti-clericalism. Once again Puccini accepted this without modification from Sardou. The caricature figure of the sacristan ('If you can mortify a heathen, then you're granted an indulgence') of course belongs to a venerable tradition of literary writing, particularly strong in Italy, home of the Papacy, but common to all western European countries. Historically, in a broad sense, the liberal hostility to what were regarded as clerically-inspired corrupting superstitions was an inherent part of the revolutionary message. Indeed anti-clericalism — in the sense of a generic hostility to the rule of priests and a readiness to crack jokes at their expense — was certainly widespread in the Papal states and predated the jacobins by some centuries; it is enough to think of Machiavelli and Guicciardini. But recent historical research has shown that, in the specific context of the jacobin years in Italy, Sardou for once was not wholly accurate. The Italian jacobins, in fact, throughout Italy but especially in Rome, were particularly cautious in their attitude towards the Church, precisely because of its hold on the peasant masses. Sardou could hardly have known of this, and it was eminently natural for a French intellectual of the 1880s, schooled in the disputes between Church and State, to assume a historical identity between liberal revolution and anti-clericalism as a contrast to that reactionary, clerical rule of the backward governments of Naples and Rome, which in the Restoration years would be subsumed in the phrase 'throne and altar'.

For Puccini, this anti-clericalism would have come naturally. Although Lucca, his birthplace, was traditionally a 'clerical' town, perhaps through its determination to assert its independence from the surrounding anti-clerical Tuscany, Puccini had been educated in a liberal state which Pius XI and his successors had refused to recognise. Only a few years before Puccini wrote *Tosca*, the authoritarian, anti-clerical reforming prime minister Crispi had been responsible for a penal code which abolished the death penalty (so prominent in *Tosca*) and punished 'clerical abuses'. In the anti-clericalism that permeates *Tosca*, the personal and cultural experiences of Puccini, as youth and man, join naturally with the inspiration he drew from Sardou.

29

Thematic Guide

Many of the themes from the opera have been identified in the articles by numbers in square brackets, which refer to the themes set out on these pages. The themes are also identified by the numbers in brackets at the corresponding points in the libretto, so that the words can be related to the musical themes.

[1] *Scarpia*
Andante molto sostenuto
fff *tutta forza*

[2]
Vivacissimo con violenza
ff

[3] *Angelotti's sister*
Vivacissimo con violenza
f

[4] *The Sacristan*
Allegretto grazioso
p

[5]
Allegretto grazioso
p

[6]
Andante moderato
p

[7] *Tosca*
Andante moderato
a

[8] **CAVARADOSSI**

How strange a thing is beau - ty
Re - con - di - ta ar - mo - ni - a

[9] **CAVARADOSSI**

So dark my Flo - ri - a
E bru - na, Flo - ri - a

[10] **CAVARADOSSI**

And you my gold - en beau - ty
E te bel - ta - dei i - gno - - ta, __

[11] *Angelotti*

[12] **ANGELOTTI**

I have es - caped from Ca - stel San - t'An - ge - lo ...
Fug - gii pur o - ra da Ca - stel San - t'An - ge - lo ...

[13]

[14] **TOSCA**

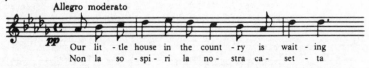

Our lit - tle house in the coun - try is wait - ing
Non la so - spi - ri la no - stra ca - set - ta

[15] **CAVARADOSSI**

What eyes in all the world can e - qual
Qua - l'oc - chio al mon - do puo star __ di pa - ro

[16]

Allegro con spirito

[17] **SACRISTAN**

Allegro con spirito *tratt.*

tornando a tempo

We are to have a torch-light pro-cess-ion

E que-sta se-ra gran fiac-co-la-ta,

[18]

Andante mosso

BELLS

[19]

Largo religioso sostenuto molto

[20]

Andante

[21]

Tempo di Gavotta molto moderato

[22] **SCARPIA**

Andante un po' agitato

Rich-er far is the flav-our of a vi-o-lent con-quest

Ha più for-te sa-po-re__ la con-qui-sta vio-len-ta

[23]

Andante mosso

[23a]

[24] Lento

[25] Andante sostenuto

[26] **TOSCA**
Andante mosso

Ah!__ This tor-ture must cease. It's more than I can bear
Ah!__ ces - sa-te il mar-tir!__ e trop - po sof-frir!__

[27] **CAVARADOSSI**
Allegro concitato

God of ven-geance ap-pear,
L'al - ba vin - di-ce ap - par

[28] **SCARPIA**
Allegro vivace

Ah, you off - er a bribe
Gia mi di - con ve - nal,

[29] Allegro vivace

[30] **SCARPIA**
Andante appassionato molto

How I have ached with love for the di - va!
Gia __ mi __ strug - gea l'a - mor del - la di - va!

[31] Allegro DRUMS

col 8va

[32] **TOSCA**
Andante lento appassionato *dolcissimo con grande sentimento*

Life has taught me sing - ing and lov - ing
Vis - si d'ar - te, vis - si d'a - mo - re,

33

[33] Andante sostenuto

[34] Andante sostenuto

[35] **SHEPHERD BOY**

Andante molto sostenuto

No word can cheer me _____ My heart is sad and
Io de' so-spi-ri, _____ Te ne ri-man-no

hea-vy_____
tan-ti,_____

[36] Andante lento appassionato molto

rit. *rubando* *rit.* *a tempo*

[37] **CAVARADOSSI**

Andantino sostenuto

teneramente

Oh hands of mer-cy, in-no-cent and lov-ing
O dol-ci ma-ni man-su-e-te e pu-re

[38] Andantino moderatamente mosso

[39] **TOSCA AND CAVARADOSSI**

Andante sostenuto / *con grande entusiasmo*

World of love shin-ing with pro-mise fla-ming with pas-sion
Tri-on-fal _____ di no-va spe-me l'a-ni-ma fre-me

[40] Largo con gravità

34

Tosca

Text by Giuseppe Giacosa and Luigi Illica
after the play by Victorien Sardou
English Translation by Edmund Tracey

Tosca was first performed at the Teatro Costanzi, Rome, on January 14, 1900. It was first performed in England at Covent Garden on July 12, 1900 and in the USA on February 4, 1901 at the Metropolitan, New York.

This translation was commissioned for a new production by English National Opera at the London Coliseum on February 4, 1976.

The stage directions follow the original published libretto, and do not describe any actual production. The text that Puccini actually set to music often varies from the libretto Ricordi published in 1905 opposite W. Beatty-Kingston's translation. This text follows the verse layout devised by Giacosa and Illica but incorporates all the final text.

THE CHARACTERS

Floria Tosca *a famous singer*	*soprano*
Mario Cavaradossi *a painter*	*tenor*
Baron Scarpia *Chief of Police*	*baritone*
Cesare Angelotti	*bass*
Sacristan	*baritone*
Spoletta *a police official*	*tenor*
Sciarrone *an agent*	*bass*
A Gaoler	*bass*
A Shepherd-boy	*contralto / treble*
Roberti *the executioner*	*non-speaking*
A Cardinal, A Judge	
A Secretary, An Officer	*parts*

Choirboys, Citizens, Acolytes, Priests, Police Agents, Guards, Soldiers

Rome, June 1800.

Act One

The church of Sant'Andrea della Valle.

(On the right: the Attavanti Chapel. On the left: scaffolding: on it, a large picture covered by a cloth. Painter's equipment. A basket.)

ANGELOTTI
(in ragged prison clothes, dishevelled, and trembling with fear. He enters panting, almost running, [2] through the side door. He glances rapidly about him.)

Ah! Here in safety! I'm in such a panic,	Ah! . . . Finalmente! . . . Nel terror mio stolto
I'm suspicious of everyone who passes.	vedea ceffi di birro in ogni volto.

(He turns and looks carefully around him, more calmly, to get his bearings. He gives a sigh of relief as he sees the column with the holy water stoup and the Madonna.)

The font . . . And the column . . . [3]	La pila . . . la colonna . . .
"The foot of the Madonna"	"A piè della Madonna"
is where my sister told me . . .	mi scrisse mia sorella . . .

(He approaches it, searches around the feet of the Madonna, and, with a suppressed cry of joy, picks up a key.)

Here is the key . . . and that must be the Chapel!	Ecco la chiave . . . ed ecco la Cappella! . . .

(Crossing to the Attavanti Chapel, with great caution he slips the key into the lock, opens the gate, passes inside the Chapel, closes the gate . . . and disappears.)

SACRISTAN
(entering from the back, with a bundle of paint-brushes in his hands, and talking loudly as though addressing someone) [4, 5]

I'm always cleaning! . . . cleaning his filthy brushes.	E frega e lava! . . . Ogni pennello è sozzo
Who would have thought a painter would make such messes!	peggio che il collarin d'uno scagnozzo.
God bless your honour . . . No!	Signor pittore . . . Tò! . . .

(He looks across to the scaffolding where the picture is, and seeing no-one there gives an exclamation of surprise.)

Deserted. I'll take my oath	Nessuno. – Avrei giurato
he was here just now: I heard him.	che fosse ritornato
No! Cavalier Cavaradossi.	il cavalier Cavaradossi.

(He puts down the brushes, climbs onto the scaffolding, looks into the basket, and says:)

No,	No,
I'm dreaming. He's not had his lunch yet.	sbaglio. – Il paniere è intatto.

(The Angelus sounds. The sacristan kneels and humbly prays.)

Angelus Domini nuntiavit Mariae,	Angelus Domini nuntiavit Mariae,
Et concepit de Spiritu Sancto.	Et concepit de Spiritu Sancto.
Ecce ancilla Domini;	Ecce ancilla Domini;
Fiat mihi secundum Verbum tuum	Fiat mihi secundum Verbum tuum
Et Verbum caro factum est	Et Verbum caro factum est
Et habitavit in nobis . . .	Et habitavit in nobis . . .

Cavaradossi – Sacristan

CAVARADOSSI
(from the side door, seeing the sacristan kneeling)

At prayer?	Che fai?

SACRISTAN
(rising)

Saying the *Angelus*.	Recito l'*Angelus*.

(Cavaradossi climbs onto the scaffolding and uncovers the picture. It is a Mary Magdalene with large blue eyes and a great mass of golden hair. [6, 7a] The painter stands in front of it, silently, examining it. The sacristan, turning to Cavaradossi to speak to him, sees the uncovered picture and exclaims in amazement.)

Holy Virgin!   O sante
How do you know her?   ampolle! Il suo ritratto! . . .

CAVARADOSSI

Know who?   Di chi?

SACRISTAN

That strange young lady: Di quell'ignota
these last few mornings before the Madonna   che i di passati a pregar qui venia
praying with such devotion . . .   tutta devota – e pia.
(He points towards the Madonna where Angelotti found the key.)

CAVARADOSSI
(smiling)

You saw her! She was so rapt   È vero. E tanto ell'era
in contemplation praying with such fervour,   infervorato nella sua preghiera
so I borrowed her likeness; she never saw me.   ch'io ne pinsi, non visto, il bel sembiante.

SACRISTAN
(to himself)

(Satan, get thee behind me!)   (Fuori, Satana, fuori!)

CAVARADOSSI

Here take my palette!   Dammi i colori!

(The sacristan obeys. Cavaradossi paints rapidly, frequently stopping to inspect his work. The sacristan goes off and returns with a small bowl, in which he continues his job of washing the brushes. All of a sudden Cavaradossi stops painting; he takes from his pocket a medallion containing a miniature, and his eyes go from the medallion to the picture.)

How strange a thing is beauty,   [8]   Recondita armonia
in its differing faces! . . . So dark my Floria,   [9]   di bellezze diverse! . . . È bruna Floria,
so passionate and loving.   l'ardente amante mia,
And you, my golden beauty,   [10]   e te, beltade ignota . . .
in your innocent sweetness!   cinta di chiome bionde!
You have smiling blue eyes, Tosca's blaze   Tu azzurro hai l'occhio e Tosca ha l'occhio
    so darkly!   nero!
Art is a strange enigma,   L'arte nel suo mistero
with the power to blend all kinds of beauty;   le diverse bellezze insiem confonde:
but though I paint the fair one,   ma nel ritrar costei
all my thoughts are of Tosca.   il mio solo pensiero, Tosca sei tu!

SACRISTAN
(muttering to himself)

(To hear this heathen scorn the laws of   (Scherza coi fanti e lascia stare i santi . . .
    heaven . . .
They're all the same,   Queste diverse gonne
these women, who think they can compete   che fanno concorrenza alle Madonne
    with the Madonna.
They all stink of the devil!   mandan tanfo d'inferno.
Free-thinking dogs, atheists and schemers,   Ma con quei cani – di volterriani
who set themselves against the Holy Office!   nemici del santissimo governo
A parcel of incorrigible sinners!   non c'è da metter voce! . . .
So let us make the sign against the devil.)   Facciam piuttosto il segno della croce.)
(to Cavaradossi)
I'll be off now, may I?   Eccellenza, vado?

CAVARADOSSI

Yes, if you wish to!   Fa il tuo piacere!
(He returns to his painting.)

SACRISTAN
(pointing at the basket)

You haven't eaten . . .   Pieno è il paniere . . .

37

Can you be fasting?	Fa penitenza?

CAVARADOSSI

No, I'm not hungry.	Fame non ho.

SACRISTAN
(ironically, rubbing his hands)

Oh . . . I'm sorry!	Oh! . . . mi rincresce!

(*He cannot refrain from making a gleeful gesture and glancing greedily at the basket, which he places to one side.*)

Mind you lock up when leaving.	Badi, quand'esce chiuda.

CAVARADOSSI

Yes!	Va!

SACRISTAN

So!	Vo.

(*He leaves at the back. Cavaradossi returns to work, his back to the Chapel. Angelotti, thinking the church is empty, appears at the gate and puts the key in the lock to open it.*)

Cavaradossi – Angelotti

CAVARADOSSI
(turning, as he hears the key in the lock)

Someone's inside there!	[2] Gente là dentro!

(*Angelotti, panic-stricken by Cavaradossi's movement, looks as though he is about to go back into the Chapel – but – raising his eyes, he exclaims in joy and then fearfully tries to stifle his cry. He has recognised the painter, and stretches his arms out to him, as to an unexpected friend in need.*) [11]

ANGELOTTI

You Cavaradossi!	Voi! Cavaradossi!
God sent you to me!	Vi manda Iddio!

(crossing to the foot of the scaffolding)

Am I so much altered?	Non mi ravvisate?
Has prison changed my face so you don't know me?	Il carcere mi ha dunque assai mutato!

CAVARADOSSI

(*He stares intently at Angelotti's face, and finally recognises him. He quickly puts down his palette and brushes and comes down from the scaffolding towards Angelotti, looking cautiously about him.*)

Angelotti!	Angelotti!
The Roman Republic's noble and persecuted Consul.	Il Console della spenta repubblica romana.

(He runs to close the door on the right.)

ANGELOTTI

I have escaped from Castel Sant'Angelo . . .	[12] Fuggii pur ora da Castel Sant'Angelo . . .

CAVARADOSSI

I am yours to command.	Disponete di me.

TOSCA
(off-stage)

Mario!	Mario!

(At the sound of Tosca's voice, Cavaradossi motions to Angelotti to be quiet.)

CAVARADOSSI

Go hide yourself!	Celatevi!
She is terribly jealous. I'll send her off in just a moment.	È una donna . . . gelosa. Un breve istante e la rimando.

38

TOSCA
(off-stage)

Mario!   Mario!

CAVARADOSSI
(in the direction of her voice)

Here I am!   Eccomi!

ANGELOTTI
(Suddenly overcome with weakness, he leans against the scaffolding.)

I am   Sono
faint with exhaustion and with hunger . . .   stremo di forze – non mi reggo.

CAVARADOSSI
(He hastily fetches the basket from the scaffolding, and half helps and half pushes Angelotti towards the Chapel.)

This basket [11]   In questo
will soon revive you; there's wine too.   panier vi è cibo e vino.

ANGELOTTI

Thank you!   Grazie!

CAVARADOSSI

Quickly!   Presto!

(Angelotti enters the Chapel.)

———————

Cavaradossi – Tosca

TOSCA
(off-stage, calling repeatedly, in irritation)

Mario!   Mario!

CAVARADOSSI
(He opens the door.)

I'm here.   Son qui!

TOSCA
(She enters almost violently, brusquely pushes Mario away as he tries to embrace her, and looks suspiciously around.) [13]

Locked and bolted?   [11]   Perchè chiuso?

CAVARADOSSI

The sacristan   Lo vuole
insisted . . .   il Sagrestano.

TOSCA

I heard you talking . . .   A chi parlavi?

CAVARADOSSI

To you!   A te!

TOSCA

To someone else; I heard you whisper.   Altre parole bisbigliavi. Ov'è? . . .
She's here.   passi e un fruscio di vesti . . .

CAVARADOSSI

Who?   Chi?

TOSCA

Don't lie. It's a woman!   Colei! . . . Quella donna! . . .
I heard her rapid steps   Ho udito i lesti
and her silken dress was rustling . . .   passi e un fruscio di vesti . . .

CAVARADOSSI

Nonsense!   Sogni!

39

You swear it?   Lo neghi?

CAVARADOSSI

I swear I love you!   Lo nego e t'amo!
(He tries to kiss her.)

TOSCA
(gently reproachful)

Oh! Before the Holy Virgin . . .   Oh! innanzi la Madonna . . .
No, Mario dear, let me pray for a moment,   Lascia pria ch'io l'infiori e che la preghi.
  with my flowers.
*(She goes over to the Madonna, skilfully arranges the flowers she has brought with her around
the statue, kneels and prays with great devotion* [13]; *then she rises to address Cavaradossi,
who has returned to his work.)*
Mario, listen to me . . . Tonight I'm singing,   Ora stammi a sentir – stassera canto,
but I finish quite early. When it's over,   ma è spettacolo breve. – Tu m'aspetti
come round the stage and meet me,   sull'uscio della scena
we'll drive down to your villa, we'll be   e alla tua villa andiam soli, soletti.
  alone there.

CAVARADOSSI
(his thoughts elsewhere)

This evening?   [2] Stassera?!

TOSCA

The moon is full,   È luna piena
the heavy scent of flowers fills the air   ed il notturno effluvio floreal
and charms the heart. Don't you feel happy?   inebria il cor. – Non sei contento?

CAVARADOSSI
(still rather absent-mindedly and hesitantly)

Happy!   Tanto!

TOSCA
(struck by his tone)

Say it once more!   Tornalo a dir!

CAVARADOSSI

Happy!   Tanto!

TOSCA

I don't believe you.   Lo dici male!
(She sits on the steps close to Cavaradossi.)
Our little house in the country is waiting,   Non la sospiri la nostra casetta
the shady garden for ever inviting.   che tutta ascosa nel verde ci aspetta?
No-one has seen our pretty olive grove,   nido a noi sacro, ignoto al mondo inter,
place of secrets and of love.   pien d'amore e di mister.
  We shall hear in the stillness,   Al tuo fianco sentire
    through the starlit spaces,   per le silenzïose
    the murmurs of the night,   stellate ombre, salir
    with all its delicate voices!   le voci delle cose!
  From all the woods and copses,   Dai boschi, dai roveti,
    from parching meadows, from towers,   dall'arse erbe, dall'imo
    from tombs of vanished glory   dei franti sepolcreti
    all scented with flowers,   odorosi di timo,
  the whispers of the night   la notte escon bisbigli
    go out from one to another   di minuscoli amori
    and often promise falsely   e perfidi consigli
    vows that melt every lover.   che ammolliscono i cuori.
Oh blossom all you meadows, fresh sea   Fiorite, o campi immensi, palpitate
  breezes,
gently caress me, shine on us sweetly,   aure marine nel lunar albor,
  silver moon above.
Ah, you starry vaults of night, let passion   Ah, piovete voluttà, vôlte stellate!
  rain down!
Tosca burns with ardent love!   Arde in Tosca un folle amor!

40

CAVARADOSSI
(won over, but cautious)

Ah, you bind me with your fetters, my [14] Ah! Mi avvinci ne'tuoi lacci mia sirena!
beloved.
My beloved, I'm yours!   Mia sirena!...verrò.
(He looks towards Angelotti's hiding place.)
Now you must let me finish.   [2] Or lasciami al lavoro.

TOSCA

You don't want me?   Mi discacci?

CAVARADOSSI

It's important, you know!   Urge l'opra, lo sai!

TOSCA

I'm going, I'm going!   Vado! Vado!
(She raises her eyes, and she notices the picture.)
But who is that   Chi è quella
golden vision just there?   donna bionda lassù?

CAVARADOSSI

The Magdalena.   La Maddalena.
You like it?   Ti piace?

TOSCA

She's too attractive!   È troppo bella!

CAVARADOSSI
(laughing and bowing)

You praise me highly.   Prezioso elogio.

TOSCA
(suspiciously)

Do I?   Ridi?
I've seen those sky-blue eyes before, I'll   Quegli occhi cilestrini già li vidi ...
swear it ...

CAVARADOSSI
(unconcerned)

Oh, you must have seen many!   Ce n'è tanti pel mondo!

TOSCA
(trying to remember)

I know her! ... I know her! ...   Aspetta ... Aspetta ...
Young Attavanti!   È l'Attavanti!

CAVARADOSSI
(laughing)

Bravo!   Brava!

TOSCA
(blind with jealousy)

You know her? Love her? She loves you? [11] La vedi? T'ama? Tu l'ami? Tu l'ami?
You love her?
Those whispers, those rustling footsteps ...   Quei pasi e quel bisbiglio ...
Ah, just now she was with you!   Ah ... Qui stava pur ora!

CAVARADOSSI

Please listen!   Vien via!

TOSCA

Ah, what a harlot! You're false to me!   Ah! la civetta! A me, a me!

CAVARADOSSI
(now serious)

She comes here daily, kneels to the   La vidi ieri – ma fu puro caso.
Madonna,

41

prays with deep devotion, she never even saw me.

A pregar qui venne . . . non visto la ritrassi.

TOSCA

Swear it.

Giura!

CAVARADOSSI
(*still serious*)

I swear it.

Giuro!

TOSCA
(*still staring at the picture*)

See how she stares intently!

Come mi guarda fiso!

CAVARADOSSI
(*He gently pushes her, so that she starts to go down the steps – backwards, her hands in Cavaradossi's, above her. As she descends she continues to face the picture, to which Mario's back is turned.*)

My dearest!

Vien via . . .

TOSCA

She laughs at me and scorns me.

Di me, beffarda, ride.

(*They have reached the bottom of the steps.*)

CAVARADOSSI

What nonsense!

Follia!

(*He holds her close to him and gazes at her.*)

TOSCA
(*insistently*)

Ah! Those eyes! . . .

Ah, quegli occhi! . . .

CAVARADOSSI

What eyes in all the world can equal those dark fiery eyes of my Tosca?
In them I find myself. My life and being are only for Tosca.
Eyes that in love are tender then blaze with anger.
What eyes can ever be found to equal the dark eyes of Tosca?

[15] Quale occhio al mondo può star di paro all'ardente occhio tuo nero?
È qui che l'esser mio s'affisa intero.

Occhio all'amor soave, all'ira fiero . . .

qual'altro al mondo può star di paro all'occhio tuo nero?

TOSCA
(*Entranced, she rests her head on Cavaradossi's shoulder.*)

You know the way to conquer my heart and soul for ever! . . .

Oh come la sai bene l'arte di farti amare! . . .

(*still pursuing her same theme*)

But make her eyes look darker!

Ma . . . falle gli occhi neri!

CAVARADOSSI

Why so jealous?

Mia gelosa!

TOSCA

Yes, I know it, I torment you night and morning.

Si, lo sento . . . ti tormento senza posa.

CAVARADOSSI

Why so jealous?

Mia gelosa!

TOSCA

But I'm certain you'd forgive me, if you knew all the pain of my love!

Certa son – del perdono se tu guardi al mio dolor!

CAVARADOSSI

Tosca, dearest goddess,

[7] Mia Tosca idolatra,

I adore your every passion;	Ogni cosa in te mi piace;
wild fits of anger	l'ira audace
or the ecstasy of love!	e lo spasimo d'amor!

TOSCA

Whisper slowly [7]	Dilla ancora
sweetest words that can console me ...	la parola che consola ...
Tell me, tell me!	dilla ancora!

CAVARADOSSI

My dearest love, my jealous Tosca, [7]	Sì, mia vita, amante inquieta,
I shall always love you.	dirò sempre: "Floria, t'amo!"
Ah! Calm your envy,	Ah! l'alma acquieta
for my love is all for you!	Sempre "T'amo!" ti dirò!

TOSCA
(breaking away, frightened of being wholly won over)

| Oh! What are you doing? | Dio! quante peccata! |
| My hair is in confusion. | M'hai tutta spettinata. |

CAVARADOSSI

Now go, I must work!   Or va – lasciami!

TOSCA

Well stay till this evening	Tu fino a stassera
and finish the picture. Make me a promise:	stai fermo al lavoro. E mi prometti
you'll talk to no women,	sia caso o fortuna,
not blue-eyed nor black-eyed,	sia treccia bionda o bruna,
no matter where they pray. Promise me,	a pregar non verrà, donna nessuna?
Mario.	

CAVARADOSSI

My love, I promise! Go!   Lo giuro, amore! ... – Va!

TOSCA

Why all this hurry?   Quanto m'affretti!

CAVARADOSSI
(gently reproachful, seeing her jealousy flare again)

Not trust me?   Ancora?

TOSCA
(falling into his arms and offering him her cheek)

Yes, forgive me!   No – perdona!

CAVARADOSSI
(smiling)

Before the Holy Virgin?   Davanti la Madonna?

TOSCA

She understands us!   È tanto buona!
(One kiss, and Tosca hurries away.)

Cavaradossi – Angelotti

(Cavaradossi listens to Tosca's footsteps receding in the distance, then very carefully opens the door and looks out. Seeing that all is clear, he runs to the Chapel. Angelotti immediately appears at the gate.) [2]

CAVARADOSSI
(opening the gate for Angelotti, who of course must have overheard the preceding conversation)

My Tosca is so honest she believes	È buona la mia Tosca, ma credente
she has to tell all she knows in confession.	al confessor nulla tien celato,
I tell her nothing. We have to tread with	ond'io mi tacqui. È cosa più prudente.
caution.	

ANGELOTTI

We're alone here?   Siam soli?

CAVARADOSSI

Yes. Now tell me what your plan is.   Si. Qual'è il vostro disegno?

ANGELOTTI

I have a simple choice: to leave the country, [3] A norma degli eventi, uscir di Stato
or stay in Rome in hiding. My young   o star celato in Roma. Mia sorella . . .
sister . . .

CAVARADOSSI

The Attavanti?   L'Attavanti?

ANGELOTTI

        Yes. She's brought woman's   Si . . . ascose un muliebre
clothing and concealed it there, under the   abbigliamento là sotto l'altare . . .
altar . . .
bonnet, dress, cloak, a fan. I'll put them on vesti, velo, ventaglio. Appena imbruni
as soon as night has fallen . . .   indosserò quei panni . . .

CAVARADOSSI

        Now I follow! [6]   Or comprendo!
Such cautious prudence in her air,   Quel fare circospetto
such continual praying   e il pregante fervore
in one so young and lovely   in giovin donna e bella
aroused my deep suspicions   m'avean messo in sospetto
of some forbidden love!   di qualche occulto amor! . . .
Now I follow!   Or comprendo!
Purest love of a sister!   Era amor di sorella!

ANGELOTTI

She stopped at nothing   Tutto ella ha osato
to rescue me from Scarpia, cursed monster. [1] onde sottrarmi a Scarpia scellerato!

CAVARADOSSI

Scarpia? That dirty bigot who beneath the   Scarpia?! Bigotto satiro che affina
cloak of religion
gratifies his squalid lusts and passions.   colle devote pratiche – la foia
He can bend   libertina – e strumento
to his evil ambition   al lascivo talento
churchman as well as hangman!   fa il confessore e il boia!
Whatever it may cost me, I'll save your life! La vita mi costasse, vi salverò!
But to stay here till nightfall is too risky. Ma indugiar fino a notte è mal sicuro.

ANGELOTTI

I fear the daylight.   Temo del sole!

CAVARADOSSI
(pointing)

        From this Chapel you will come   La Cappella mette
to an orchard, then to a stream which   ad un orto mal chiuso – indi un canneto
winds along
through the meadows to my villa . . .   mena lungi pei campi a una mia villa.

ANGELOTTI

I know it . . .   Mi è nota.

CAVARADOSSI

Here is the door key . . . I will rejoin you   Ecco la chiave – innanzi sera
there this evening; now, where did you say   io vi raggiungo – portate con voi
are the things your sister left you?   le vesti femminili.

ANGELOTTI
(He picks up the bundle of clothes under the altar.)

        Shall I wear them?   Ch'io le indossi?

There is no need for now the path is deserted ...

Per or non monta, il sentiero è deserto.

ANGELOTTI
(about to go)

God bless you!

Addio!

CAVARADOSSI
(running over to Angelotti)

If anything happens there is a well
in the garden. It is a deep one,
but halfway down a small narrow passage
leads inside to a secret cavern;
it's absolutely safe and no-one knows it!

Se urgesse il periglio, correte
al pozzo del giardin. L'acqua è nel fondo,
ma a mezzo della canna un picciol varco
guida ad un antro oscuro,
rifugio impenetrabile e sicuro!

(A cannon-shot; they look at each other in alarm.) [2]

ANGELOTTI

The alarm from the castle!

Il cannon del castello!

CAVARADOSSI

Your escape
is discovered! Now Scarpia will loose all
his rabble!

Fu scoperta
la fuga! Or Scarpia i suoi sbirri sguinzaglia!

ANGELOTTI

Good-bye, friend!

Addio!

CAVARADOSSI
(with sudden resolve)

I'm coming too. We must be careful.

Con voi verrò. Staremo all'erta!

ANGELOTTI

Someone is here!

Odo qualcun!

CAVARADOSSI
(enthusiastically)

Fight to the death if we're challenged!

Se ci assalgon, battaglia!

(They leave quickly through the Chapel.)

Sacristan – Pupils and Choristers of the Chapel – Acolytes – Penitents

SACRISTAN
(He enters hurriedly in a fluster, shouting.) [4, 5]

Joyful tidings, your Excellency!

Sommo giubilo, Eccellenza! ...

(Looking over to the scaffolding, he is surprised that once again the artist is not there.)

He's not here. I'm really sorry.
If you can mortify a heathen,
you are granted an indulgence!

Non c'è più! Ne son dolente!!
Chi contrista un miscredente
si guadagna un'indulgenza!

(Acolytes, penitents, and pupils and choristers of the Chapel run in from all directions. There is general hubbub and chaos.)

All the choir in here at once!
Quickly!

Tutta qui la cantoria!
Presto! ...

(More choirboys come in, late. Eventually all are present.) [16]

PUPILS
(in complete turmoil)

What then?

Dove?

SACRISTAN

Come on, don't dawdle ...

In sagrestia.

(He pushes some of the acolytes along.)

What has happened?   Ma che avvenne?

SACRISTAN

Haven't they told you?   Nol sapete?
Bonaparte ... The scoundrel ...   Bonaparte ... scellerato ...
Bonaparte ...   Bonaparte ...

OTHER PUPILS

Go on! Go on!   Ebben? Che fu?

SACRISTAN

He was plucked and drawn and quartered.   Fu spennato, sfracellato
Now he's boiling in a pot.   e piombato a Belzebù!

PUPILS, CHORISTERS, ETC.

What's he saying?   Chi lo dice?
Imagination!   – È sogno! – È fola!

SACRISTAN

It is perfect truth I tell you.   È veridica parola
They have just received dispatches.   or ne giunse la notizia!
We are to have   [17]   E questa sera
a torchlight procession,   gran fiaccolata,
also a gala tonight at the Palace.   veglia di gala a Palazzo Farnese,
For the occasion   ed un'apposita
a new cantata   nuova cantata
with Floria Tosca!   con Floria Tosca!
And in the churches   E nelle chiese
hymns to the Lord!   inni al Signor!
Now get ready   Or via a vestirvi,
and stop this noise!   non più clamore!
     Via, via in sagrestia!

ALL
(laughing and shouting gaily)

Double money ... *Te Deum* ... *Gloria!* [16,17] Doppio soldo ... *Te Deum* ... *Gloria!*
Praise the King! ... Great Victorious   Viva il Re! ... Si festeggi la vittoria!
  celebrations!

Scarpia – Sacristan – Choristers, Pupils, etc.– Spoletta– Police Agents

(When their shouting and laughter reach their height, an ironic voice cuts harshly through the raucous tumult of songs and mirth. It is Scarpia; behind him, Spoletta and a number of police agents.) [1]

SCARPIA

You make the church a fairground! More   Un tal baccano in chiesa! Bel rispetto!
  decorum!

SACRISTAN
(stammering with fear)

Your Excellency, the great victory ...   Eccellenza, il gran giubilo ...

SCARPIA

Are you ready   Apprestate
for the *Te Deum?*   per il *Te Deum.*

(They all slink away: the sacristan is also on the point of disappearing when Scarpia brusquely detains him.)

Stay here, you!   Tu resta!

SACRISTAN
(frightened)

I'm not moving!   Non mi muovo!

And you go, ferret out everything,
and search every corner!

E tu va, fruga ogni angolo, raccogli
ogni traccia!

SPOLETTA

At once, sir!   Sta bene!
(*He motions two agents to follow him.*)

SCARPIA
(*to other agents*)

Guard every entrance,   Occhio alle porte,
don't arouse suspicion!   ma senza dar sospetti!
(*to the sacristan*)
As for you. Ponder   Ora a te. Pesa
before you answer. A prisoner of State   [12] le tue risposte.Un prigionier di Stato
has just escaped from Castel Sant'Angelo ...   pur or fuggito di Castel Sant'Angelo
He sought a refuge here.   s'è rifugiato qui.

SACRISTAN

Oh God protect us!   Misericordia!

SCARPIA

Maybe he's here still. Now where's the   Forse c'è ancora. Dov'è la Cappella
    Chapel
of the Attavanti?   degli Attavanti?

SACRISTAN

Here it is!   Eccola!
(*He goes to the gate and notices it is unlocked.*)
It's open! You saints above!   Aperta! Arcangeli!
Here's a new key too!   E ... un'altra chiave!

SCARPIA

How intriguing ... We'll go in then.   Buon indizio. Entriamo.

(*They go into the Chapel, then return: Scarpia is considerably annoyed. In his hands he has a
closed fan, which he plays with restlessly.*) [12, 2]

It was a grave error   Fu grave sbaglio
firing off the cannon. The bird flew up   quel colpo di cannone. Il mariolo
and away from our clutches. Here's a fan   spiccato ha il volo, ma lasciò una preda ...
    that may guide us ...
Whose is it? This fan!   prezïosa – un ventaglio.
Who helped him to escape   Qual complice il misfatto
our close pursuit?   preparò?

(*He remains deep in thought, then scrutinises the fan; suddenly he notices the crest.*)

The Marchesa   La marchesa
Attavanti! It's her crest!   Attavanti! ... Il suo stemma ...

(*He looks around, searching every corner of the church: his attention is caught by the
scaffolding, the painter's materials, the picture ... and the celebrated Attavanti face looking
at him in the face of the saint.*)

And that's her portrait! [10]   Il suo ritratto!
(*to the sacristan*)
You know who did this picture?   Chi fe' quelle pitture?

SACRISTAN

The Cavalier [6]   Il cavaliere
Cavaradossi ...   Cavaradossi.

SCARPIA

Ah!   Lui!

(*One of the agents comes back from the Chapel carrying the basket Cavaradossi gave
Angelotti.*)

47

SACRISTAN
(seeing it)

Heavens! There's his basket! | Numi! Il paniere!

SCARPIA
(pursuing his own train of thought)

So! The lover of Tosca! He's on our black list. | Lui! L'amante di Tosca! Un uom sospetto!
Believes in Voltaire! | Un volterrian!

SACRISTAN
(who has gone over to inspect the basket)

Empty! Empty! | Vuoto? Vuoto!

SCARPIA

What is it? | Che hai detto?
(He sees the agent with the basket.)
Come on! | Che fu?

SACRISTAN
(taking the basket)

He found this basket in the Chapel, [4] this fellow here. | Si ritrovè nella Cappella questo panier.

SCARPIA

Is it familiar? | Tu lo conosci?

SACRISTAN

Very! | Certo!
(He stammers with fear.)
The painter brings it here. But, if I may, sir... | È il cesto del pittor...ma... nondimeno...

SCARPIA

Spit it out, spit it out! | Sputa quello che sai.

SACRISTAN

I left it here myself, filled with exquisite refreshments. The painter's tasty lunch! | Io lo lasciai ripieno di cibo prelibato... il pranzo del pittore!...

SCARPIA
(attentive, seeking to discover more)

Well then, he ate it! | Avrà pranzato!

SACRISTAN

Not in the Chapel, as he hadn't a key, and, what is more, he had said he wasn't hungry. | Nella Cappella? Non ne avea la chiave nè contava pranzar...disse egli stesso.
That's why I placed the basket here in safety. | Ond'io già l'avea messo qual mia spoglia al riparo.
(Libera me Domine!) | (Libera me Domine!)
(He indicates where he left the basket.)

SCARPIA
(to himself)

(Ah, that explains it. So the sacristan's provisions fed the hungry Angelotti!) | [2] (Tutto è chiaro... la provvista – del sacrista d'Angelotti fu la preda!)
(He sees Tosca enter hurriedly.)
Tosca? I must observe her. | [7] Tosca? Che non mi veda.
(He hides behind the pillar with the holy water stoup.)
(With a handkerchief Iago drove a jealous lover to utter madness. I'll use a fan!) | (Per ridurre un geloso allo sbaraglio Jago ebbe un fazzoletto – ed io un ventaglio!)

48

TOSCA

(*She runs to the scaffolding, sure of finding Cavaradossi, and is surprised at not seeing him.*)

Mario?! Mario?!	Mario?! Mario?!

SACRISTAN
(*at the foot of the scaffolding*)

That's the gentleman	Il pittor
who painted? Who knows where he is?	Cavaradossi? Chi sa dove sia?
By witchcraft	Svani, sgattaiolò,
he was spirited away from here.	per sua stregoneria.

(*He slips out.*)

TOSCA

Has he tricked me? No . . . no . . .	Ingannata? No . . . no . . .
He won't betray our love!	tradirmi egli non può!

SCARPIA

(*He comes round the pillar. Tosca is startled by his sudden appearance. Dipping his fingers into the stoup, he offers her holy water; outside, bells ring to church.*)

Tosca, dear angel,	[18] Tosca divina
one boon I beg; my hand awaits you,	la mano mia
grace it with your fingers;	la vostra aspetta – piccola manina,
I mean no gallant gesture,	non per galanteria
but just to moisten yours with holy water.	ma per offrirvi l'acqua benedetta.

TOSCA
(*She touches Scarpia's fingers and crosses herself.*)

Thank you, my lord.	Grazie, signor!

(*The church gradually fills with townsfolk, gentry, women from the Ciociara and Trastevere quarters, soldiers, shepherds, tradesmen, beggars, etc., who congregate in the main nave: then a cardinal and the Chapter process to the high altar; the people turn towards the high altar and crowd into the main nave.*)

SCARPIA

Your lead	Un nobile
is the one we follow. With Heaven's	esempio è il vostro – al cielo
grace and its sweet inspiration,	piena di santo zelo
you revive human faith in God our Saviour	attingete dell'arte il magistero
the power of your singing!	che la fede ravviva!

TOSCA
(*preoccupied with her own thoughts*)

Kindly spoken.	Bontà vostra.

SCARPIA

Many women are worldly . . .	Le pie donne son rare . . .
Though you work in the theatre . . .	Voi calcate la scena . . .

(*significantly*)

you come to church like this, to kneel in prayer.	e in chiesa ci venite per pregar.

TOSCA
(*surprised*)

I don't follow.	Che intendete?

SCARPIA

To another	E non fate
who may look like an angel,	come certe sfrontate
visiting a church may really be	che hanno di Maddalena

(*He points to the picture.*)

shameless masking intrigues of lovers!	viso e costumi . . . e vi trescan d'amore!

TOSCA
(*suddenly aroused*)

What? Of lovers? But prove it!	Che? D'amore? Le prove!

SCARPIA
(He shows her the fan.)

A useful thing to have	È arnese di pittore
for painting ...	questo?

TOSCA
(She seizes it.)

For painting?	Un ventaglio? Dove
But where was it?	stava?

SCARPIA

There, by the canvas. Something must have [10]	Là su quel palco. Qualcun venne
startled our naughty love-bird,	certo a sturbar gli amanti
and as she flew away she lost her feathers!	ed essa nel fuggir perdè le penne!

TOSCA
(examining the fan)

The crown! The crest! The Attavanti!	La corona! Lo stemma! È l'Attavanti!
The one I suspected ...	Ah presago sospetto!

SCARPIA
(to himself)

(Now my poison is working.)	(Ho sortito l'effetto!)

TOSCA
(Barely able to hold back her tears, she forgets both where she is and whom she is with.)

I came here full of sorrow	Ed io veniva a lui tutta dogliosa
just to tell him – when evening falls	per dirgli: invan stassera
we cannot be together.	il ciel s'infosca
Tonight the lovesick Tosca	l'innamorata Tosca
is a captive! At the royal celebrations I	è prigioniera, dei regali tripudi, prigionera! ...
must glitter!	

SCARPIA
(to himself)

(Now my poison bites deeper!)	(Già il veleno l'ha rosa.)

(to Tosca, mellifluously)

Oh, what has grieved you,	[18] O che v'offende,
fairest of creatures?	dolce signora?
Why are these tears	Una ribelle
of bitterness falling	lagrima scende
over your lovely	sovra le belle
delicate features?	guancie e le irrora;
Fairest of ladies,	dolce signora,
ah, what has grieved you?	che mai v'accora?

TOSCA

Nothing!	Nulla!

SCARPIA
(ingratiatingly)

I'd lay my life down	[18] Io darei la vita
if only I could cheer you.	per asciugar quel pianto.

TOSCA
(unheeding)

I stand here weeping while	[12] Io qui mi struggo e intanto
in another's arms he makes a joke of my	d'altra in braccio le mie smanie deride!
feelings!	

SCARPIA
(to himself)

(Poison, bite deeper!)	(Morde il veleno!)

TOSCA
(in ever greater anguish)

I must know, I'd like	Dove son? Potessi

to catch them, the dirty traitors. I cannot bear it!	coglierli i traditori. Oh qual sospetto!
The villa gave refuge to two pairs of lovers.	Ai doppi amori è la villa ricetto.
To betray all our love!	Traditor! Traditor!

(in intense grief)

My pretty nest is defiled and degraded!	Oh mio bel nido insozzato di fango!

(with sudden resolve)

I'll go there now and catch them!	[2] Vi piomberò inattesa.

(She turns menacingly to the picture.)

You shall not have my Mario, I swear it.	Tu non l'avrai stassera. Giuro!

SCARPIA
(in shocked reproach)

In church!	In chiesa!

TOSCA

God will forgive me . . . For He sees how I'm weeping! . . .	Dio mi perdona. Egli vede ch'io piango!

(She leaves in great agitation [7]: Scarpia accompanies her, pretending to reassure her. No sooner has she left than he crosses back to the column and signals.)

SCARPIA
(to Spoletta, who emerges from behind the pillar)

Three agents . . . Go in a carriage, hurry!	Tre sbirri, una carozza . . . Presto – seguila
Follow wherever she leads you . . .	Dovunque vada . . . non visto . . . provvedi!
Don't lose her . . . Be careful!	

SPOLETTA

We will, sir. Where do we meet you?	Sta bene. Il convegno?

SCARPIA

Palazzo Farnese!	Palazzo Farnese!

(Spoletta hurries off with three agents.)

Go, Tosca! Now your fate is ruled by Scarpia.	Va, Tosca! Nel tuo cuor s'annida Scarpia
Go, Tosca! Now Scarpia unleashes the savage falcon	Va, Tosca! E Scarpia che scioglie a volo il falco
guarding your jealous passions. Maybe I'll [19] profit	della tua gelosia. Quanta promessa
from your doubts and suspicions!	nel tuo pronto sospetto!

CHORUS

Adjutorum nostrum in nomine Domini	Adjutorum nostrum in nomine Domini
Qui fecit coelum et terram	Qui fecit coelum et terram
Sit nomen Domini benedictum	Sit nomen Domini benedictum
Et hoc nunc et usque in saeculum.	Et hoc nunc et usque in saeculum.

SCARPIA

Two targets draw me.	A doppia mira
I must have my way. The head of this young painter	tendo il voler, nè il capo del ribelle
is a prize I long for. Ah, but to quell	è la più prezïosa. Ah, di quegli occhi
the dark imperious eyes of Tosca,	vittoriosi vedere la fiamma
see her grown faint and languish in my [19] arms,	illanguidir con spasimo d'amor,
feel her surrender, languid and faint for love . . .	fra le mie braccia illanguidir d'amor . . .
One to the gallows	L'uno al capestro,
and my arms round the other.	l'altra fra le mie braccia . . .

CHORUS

Te Deum laudamus!	Te Deum laudamus!
Te Deum confitemur!	Te Deum confitemur!

(The chanting in the background arouses him suddenly, as if from a dream. He pulls himself together, crosses himself, with a glance around him, and says:)

SCARPIA

Tosca, you turn my thoughts away from God!	Tosca, mi fai dimenticare Iddio!

(He kneels and prays fervently.)

SCARPIA, CHORUS

Te aeturnum Patrem omnis terra veneratur!	Te aeturnum Patrem omnis terra veneratur!

[1]

(Quick curtain.)

The close of Act One in the Covent Garden 1964 production (photo: Donald Southern)

Act Two

Scarpia's apartments on the upper floor of the Farnese Palace.

(The table is laid. A large window looks onto the palace courtyard. It is night.)

SCARPIA

(He is seated at the table, dining. Every so often he breaks off thoughtfully from eating. He glances at the clock: he is pensive and restless.) [20]

Tosca is a good falcon.	Tosca è un buon falco! . . .
Surely by now	Certo a quest'ora
my savage hounds have tracked them to their hiding place.	i miei segugi le due prede azzannano!
At dawn the gallows	Doman sul palco
will welcome	vedrà l'aurora
Consul Angelotti and the handsome traitor Mario!	Angelotti e il bel Mario al laccio pendere.

(He rings. Enter Sciarrone.)

Is Tosca in the Palace?	Tosca è al palazzo?

SCIARRONE

Yes, sir, a chamberlain has gone to find her.	Un ciambellan ne uscìa pur ora in traccia.

SCARPIA
(pointing to the window)

Open it. Darkness has fallen.	Apri. – Tarda è la notte.

(From the floor below –where the Queen of Naples, Maria Carolina, is giving a great reception in honour of Melas – the sound of an orchestra is heard. [21] To himself)

Still no cantata, they're waiting for Tosca, so they strum a gavotte.	Alla cantata ancor manca la Diva, e strimpellan gavotte.

(to Sciarrone)

You'd better wait for Tosca by the entrance.	Tu attenderai la Tosca in sull'entrata;
Ask her please to come here	le dirai ch'io l'aspetto
at the end of the cantata . . .	finita la cantata . . .
or better . . .	o meglio . . .

(He rises, goes to the desk and quickly scribbles a note.)

. . . go and find her with this letter.	. . . le darai questo biglietto.

(Exit Sciarrone.)

SCARPIA
(He sits down at the table again.)

She will be here . . . for her fine lover, Mario!	Ella verrà . . . per amor del suo Mario!
For her fine lover Mario she will surrender [1] to my will.	Per amor del suo Mario al piacer mio s'arrenderà. Tal dei profondi amori
People who love like Tosca find only grief and betrayal. Richer far [22]	è la profonda miseria. Ha più forte
is the flavour of a violent conquest	sapore la conquista vïolenta
than a gentle surrender. Romantic sighing	che il mellifluo consenso. Io di sospiri
and whispers in the milky moonlit dawn	e di lattiginose albe lunari
can give me no pleasure. I can't read a horoscope	poco mi appago. Non so trarre accordi
in flowers or strum a sweet guitar.	di chitarra, nè oròscopo di fiori,
I do not choose to simper	nè far l'occhio di pesce,
or to coo like a turtle-dove!	o tubar come fortora!

(rising)

53

Conquest! I conquer whatever I lust for. When I'm sated I cast it from me, turn to new sensations. God alone made different wines, different women . . . I want to taste my fill of the glorious bounty of Heaven!	Bramo. – La cosa bramata perseguo, me ne sazio e via la getto volto a nuova esca. Dio creò diverse beltà e vini diversi. Io vo' gustare quanto più posso dell'opra divina!

(He drinks.)

SCIARRONE
(entering)

Spoletta's back now.	Spoletta è giunto.

SCARPIA

Splendid! I will see him.	Entri. In buon punto.

Scarpia – Spoletta – Sciarrone

SCARPIA
(He sits down and, busy eating again, questions Spoletta without looking at him.)

Welcome, Spoletta. Did you have good hunting?	O galantuomo, come andò la caccia? . . .

SPOLETTA

(Saint Ignatius protect me!) Close on the track of the lady we followed. We found a lonely old house hidden by bushes and pine trees. She went inside and came out some time later. I gave the word to scale the wall around the garden, and we entered and stormed the villa . . .	(Sant'Ignazio mi aiuta!) Della signora seguimmo la traccia. Giunti a un'erma villetta tra le fratte perduta ella vi entrò. Ne uscì sola ben presto. Allor scavalco lesto il muro del giardin coi miei cagnotti e piombo in casa . . .

SCARPIA

My clever Spoletta!	Quel bravo Spoletta!

SPOLETTA
(faltering)

Then I scratched round . . . rummaged . . .	Fiuto! . . . razzolo! . . . frugo! . . .

SCARPIA
(He notices Spoletta's hesitation and rises to his feet, pale with fury, his brow creased in anger.)

And Angelotti?	Ahi! l'Angelotti? . . .

SPOLETTA

He wasn't there, sir!	Non s'è trovato!

SCARPIA
(in a rage)

Mongrel! You filthy traitor! That ugly snout will whimper on the gallows!	Ah cane! Ah traditore! Ceffo di basilisco, alle forche! . . .

SPOLETTA

Dear God!	Gesù!

(seeking to assuage Scarpia's wrath)

The painter was there . . .	C'era il pittore . . .

SCARPIA

Cavaradossi?	Cavaradossi?

SPOLETTA
(He nods, and immediately adds:)

He knows where the other is hiding . . . He was so scornful;	Ei sa dove l'altro s'asconde. Ogni suo gesto,

every word that he said	ogni accento, tradia
was sarcastic and mocking,	tal beffarda ironia,
it seemed wise to arrest him ...	ch'io lo trassi in arresto!

SCARPIA
(with a sigh of satisfaction)

That sounds better!   [23] Meno male!

SPOLETTA
(He points towards the ante-room.)

He is here.   Egli è là.

(Scarpia paces up and down, thinking: he stops abruptly: through the open window comes the sound of the choral cantata in the Queen's apartments.*)

SCARPIA
(to Spoletta)

Now you may bring the prisoner in.   Introducete il Cavaliere.

(Exit Spoletta. To Sciarrone)

          We'll need   A me
Roberti, and see the judge is ready.   Roberti e il Giudice del Fisco.

(Exit Sciarrone. Scarpia sits down again.)

(Spoletta and three agents lead in Mario Cavaradossi. Then Roberti, the executioner, the Exchequer Judge and Secretary, and Sciarrone.)

CAVARADOSSI
(proudly)

You insult me.   Tale violenza! ...

SCARPIA
(with studied politeness)

       Cavalier, please take a chair,   Cavalier, vi piaccia
I beg you.   accomodarvi.

CAVARADOSSI

       Tell me why ...   Vo' saper ...

SCARPIA
(pointing to a chair on the other side of the table)

         Be seated.   Sedete.

CAVARADOSSI
(refusing)

I'm waiting.   Aspetto.

SCARPIA

I see! You heard of the escape from ... [23]   E sia! – Vi è noto che un prigione ...

(Tosca's voice is heard singing in the cantata.)

---

*   **CHORUS**
       (off-stage)

Sale, ascende l'uman cantica
varca spazi, varca cèli,
per ignoti empirei,
profetati dai Vangeli,
a te giunge, o re dei re!
Questo canto voli a te.
A te questo inno voli
sommo Iddio della vittoria
Quest'inno di gloria
alle cantiche degli angeli
s'unisca e voli a te!

<table>
<tr><td colspan="2" align="center">**CAVARADOSSI**</td></tr>
<tr><td>That is Tosca!</td><td>La sua voce! ...</td></tr>
</table>

SCARPIA
(Having broken off at the sound of Tosca's voice, he now resumes.)

I'm sure you must have heard
of someone escaping from Castel Sant'
Angelo?

... vi è noto che un prigione
oggi è fuggito di Castel Sant'Angelo?

CAVARADOSSI

I heard nothing.

Ignoro.

SCARPIA

And yet it is stated that you
assisted him in Sant'Andrea, providing
him
with food and with clothing ...

Eppur si pretende che voi
l'abbiate accolto in Sant'Andrea, provvisto

di cibo e vesti ...

CAVARADOSSI
(firmly)

That's nonsense!

Menzogna!

SCARPIA
(still calm)

... and that later
you took him to your house outside the
city ...

... e guidato
ad un vostro podere suburbano.

CAVARADOSSI

Never. Now prove it.

Nego. – Le prove?

SCARPIA
(smoothly)

I have a faithful witness.

Un suddito fedele ...

CAVARADOSSI

The facts, man! Can you prove it? My
house
was ransacked, but your spies found nothing.

Al fatto. Chi mi accusa? I vostri birri

frugaro invan tutta la villa.

SCARPIA

Clearly
he's been well hidden.

Segno
che è ben celato.

CAVARADOSSI

Your spies are mistaken!

Sospetti di spia!

SPOLETTA
(taking offence)

All the time we were searching, he laughed
and mocked us ...

Alle nostre ricerche egli rideva ...

CAVARADOSSI

Of course I laughed. I'm laughing still.

E rido ancor. E rido ancor.

SCARPIA
(sharply)

Do you dare laugh at Scarpia? Be careful!
I warn you! Mark my questions!

Questo è luogo di lacrime! Badate!
Or basta! Rispondete!

(He rises and impatiently closes the window so as not to be disturbed by the singing on the floor below: then he turns imperiously to Cavaradossi.)

Where's Angelotti?

Ov'è Angelotti?

CAVARADOSSI

I don't know.

Non lo so.

SCARPIA

You gave him   Negate
a basket of provisions?   avergli dato cibo?

CAVARADOSSI

Never!   Nego!

SCARPIA

And clothing?   E vesti?

CAVARADOSSI

Never!   Nego!

SCARPIA

And refuge at your villa?   Ed asilo alla villa?

CAVARADOSSI

Never!   Nego!

SCARPIA

Where he is still hiding?   E che là sia nascosto?

CAVARADOSSI
(*emphatically*)

Never! Never!   Nego! Nego!

SCARPIA
(*cleverly, becoming calm again*)

Now, Cavaliere, do consider; all this   Via, Cavaliere, riflettete:
defiant obstinacy will not help you.   saggia non è cotesta
A prompt confession saves you   ostinatezza vostra.
from intolerable pain.   [24] Angoscia grande, pronta confessione
Let me advise you; tell me; tell me,   eviterà! Io vi consiglio, dite:
where is he hiding?   dov'è dunque Angelotti?

CAVARADOSSI

I don't know.   Non lo so.

SCARPIA

Say where   Ancor,
is Angelotti; say where!   l'ultima volta. Dov'è?

CAVARADOSSI

I don't know.   Non lo so!

SPOLETTA
(*to himself*)

(What he needs is a whipping!)   (O bei tratti di corda!)

———————

Enter Tosca, breathless.

SCARPIA
(*seeing Tosca*)

(Here she is!)   [15]   (Eccola!)

TOSCA
(*She sees Cavaradossi and runs to embrace him.*)

Mario,   Mario,
you here?!   tu qui?!

CAVARADOSSI
(*under his breath*)

(No word of what you saw today, [23]   (Di quanto là vedesti, taci
or they'll kill me! ...)   o m'uccidi! ...)

(*Tosca indicates that she has understood.*)

SCARPIA
(solemnly)

Mario Cavaradossi, the judge is waiting; you must now bear witness.

Mario Cavaradossi, qual testimonio il Giudice v'aspetta.

(to Roberti)

First the normal procedure . . . Later . . . [23] I'll instruct you.

Pria le forme ordinarie. – Indi . . . a miei cenni.

(Sciarrone opens the door leading to the torture chamber. The Judge goes in, and the others follow, except for Tosca and Scarpia. Spoletta positions himself by the door at the back of the room.) [24]

SCARPIA

Now you and I can talk like friends together. There's no need to look so frightened.

Ed or fra noi parliam da buoni amici. Via quell'aria sgomentata . . .

(He motions to Tosca to sit.)

TOSCA
(She sits down with studied calm.)

I'm perfectly at ease.

Sgomento alcun non ho.

SCARPIA

The fan is quite forgotten?

La storia del ventaglio? . . .

(Passing behind the sofa on which Tosca is seated, he leans against it, continuing with the same charm.)

TOSCA
(with feigned indifference)

It's stupid to be jealous.

Fu sciocca gelosia.

SCARPIA

The Attavanti was not installed at the villa?

L'Attavanti non era dunque alla villa?

TOSCA

No. No-one was with him.

No! Egli era solo.

SCARPIA

No-one? You're absolutely certain?

Solo? – Ne siete ben sicura?

TOSCA

I'm so easily jealous. I saw no-one!

Nulla sfugge ai gelosi. Solo! solo!

SCARPIA
(He takes a chair, places it in front of Tosca, sits on it, and looks intently at her.)

Indeed?!

Davver?

TOSCA
(irritated)

Yes, indeed!

Solo! si!

SCARPIA

So excited? Is there something you're frightened
of betraying?

Quanto fuoco! Par che abbiate paura
di tradirvi.

(calling)

Sciarrone, what does our witness say?

Sciarrone: che dice il Cavalier?

SCIARRONE
(appearing in the doorway)

Nothing.

Nega.

SCARPIA
(speaking more loudly, towards the open door)

Try him further.   Insistiamo.

(Sciarrone goes back into the torture chamber, closing the door.)

TOSCA
(laughing)

Oh, it's useless!   Oh, inutil!

SCARPIA
(He rises and paces up and down, with the utmost seriousness.)

We are only just starting.   Lo vedremo, signora.

TOSCA

Clearly, if he's to please you, he had better   Dunque per compiacervi si dovrebbe
tell lies?   mentir?

SCARPIA

Only the truth can assist him to shorten   No; ma il vero potrebbe abbreviargli un'or
hours
of horrible torture . . .   assai penosa . . .

TOSCA
(surprised)

Of horrible torture? What do you mean?   Un'ora penosa? Che vuol dir?
What's happening to Mario?   Che avviene in quella stanza?

SCARPIA

          The law must be fulfilled   È forza che si adempia
to the letter.   la legge.

TOSCA

Oh! God! But tell me what you mean . . .   Oh! Dio! . . . che avviene?

SCARPIA

          His hands and feet are bound,   Legato mani e piè
and there's a ring of iron with spikes [25]   il vostro amante ha un cerchio uncinato
around his temples.   alle tempia,
At each denial they tighten till his blood   che ad ogni niego ne sprizza sangue senza
gushes.   mercè.

TOSCA
(bounding to her feet)

Is it true? Is it true? You black-hearted   Non è ver, non è ver! Sogghigno di
murderer!   demòne . . .

(a terrible groan from Cavaradossi)

They're killing him. Oh God . . . Oh   Un gemito . . . pietà . . . pietà! . . .
God . . .

(She listens in anguish.)

SCARPIA

But you could save him.   Sta in voi salvarlo.

TOSCA

I will . . . You must stop them this minute.   Ebbene . . . ma cessate!

SCARPIA
(He goes to the door.)

          Sciarrone,   Sciarrone,
release him.   sciogliete.

SCIARRONE
(appearing in the doorway)

Completely?   Tutto?

SCARPIA

Completely.   Tutto.

(Sciarrone returns to the torture chamber and shuts the door.)

(to Tosca)
And now I want the truth.   Ed or ... la verità.

TOSCA

Let me see him! ...   Ch'io lo veda! ...

SCARPIA

No!   No!

TOSCA
(She manages to get close to the door.)

Mario!   Mario!

CAVARADOSSI
(off-stage)

Tosca!   Tosca!

TOSCA

Have they slackened   Ti straziano
the torture?   ancora?

CAVARADOSSI

Yes. Have courage – Say nothing,   No – Coraggio – Taci – Sprezzo il
nothing. I scorn the pain.   dolor.

SCARPIA
(approaching Tosca)

Come on, I want an answer.   Orsù, Tosca, parlate.

TOSCA
(She has taken heart from Cavaradossi's words.)

I know nothing.   Non so nulla!

SCARPIA

That sample   Non vale
did not move you? Roberti, we'll continue ...   la prova? ... Ripigliamo ...

TOSCA
(She stands between Scarpia and the door, to prevent him giving the order.)

No! You mustn't!   No! Fermate!

SCARPIA

Then will you tell me?   Voi parlerete? ...

TOSCA

No! No! Oh you monster ...   No! No! Ah! ... mostro!
I hate you ... You'll kill him!   lo strazi ... l'uccidi!

SCARPIA

But you are the one   Lo strazia quel vostro
who will kill him – by your silence.   silenzio assai più.

TOSCA

You're laughing –   Tu ridi ...
deriding my torment.   all'orrida pena?

SCARPIA
(with savage irony)

But Tosca was never   Mai Tosca alla scena
more tragic on stage!   più tragica fu!

(Tosca, horrified, retreats from Scarpia. With a sudden burst of ferocity he shouts loudly to Spoletta:)

Throw open the door.	Aprite le porte
Let her hear how he suffers!	che n'oda i lamenti!

(*Spoletta opens the door and stands on the threshold.*)

CAVARADOSSI
(*off-stage*)

I defy you!	Vi sfido!

SCARPIA
(*shouting to Roberti*)

Still harder! Still harder! [25]	Più forte! Più forte!

CAVARADOSSI

I defy you!	Vi sfido!

SCARPIA
(*to Tosca*)

Your answer ...	Parlate ...

TOSCA

I cannot.	Che dire?

SCARPIA

Come, tell me!	Su, via!

TOSCA

Ah! I know nothing!	Ah, non so nulla!

(*in despair*)

Do I have to lie?	Ah, dovrei mentir?

SCARPIA
(*insisting*)

Say, where is Angelotti?	Dite dov'è Angelotti?

TOSCA

No! No!	No! No!

SCARPIA

Speak up, tell me truly,	Parlate su, via
don't lie to me again.	dove celato sta?

TOSCA

Ah! This torture must cease. [26]	Ah! ... cessate il martir!
It's more than I can bear,	è troppo soffrir!
more than I can bear,	Ah! non posso più,
more than I can bear!	non posso più!

(*Once again she turns in entreaty to Scarpia, who gestures to Spoletta to let her approach: crossing to the open door, she is overwhelmed with horror at what she sees. She cries out to Cavaradossi in unbearable anguish.*)

CAVARADOSSI
(*screaming*)

Ah!	Ahimè!

TOSCA

Mario ... allow me to	O Mario, consenti
to tell him? ...	ch'io parli? ...

CAVARADOSSI
(*off-stage*)

No! No!	No! No!

TOSCA
(*insistently*)

I cannot	Ascolta,
bear any more ...	non posso più ...

CAVARADOSSI
(off-stage)

Nonsense.   Stolta,
Tell what? ... You don't know ...   che sai? ... che puoi dir? ...

SCARPIA
(Infuriated by Cavaradossi's words, and fearing Tosca may once again regain courage from them, he shouts at Spoletta:)

Now force him to be silent!   Ma fatelo tacere! ...

(Spoletta enters the torture chamber, and returns shortly afterwards, while Tosca, overcome by emotion, falls prostrate on the sofa and, sobbing, appeals to Scarpia, who remains impassive and silent. Meanwhile Spoletta is muttering a prayer under his breath. 'Judex erge cum sedebit quidquid latet apparebit nil inultum remanebit.')

TOSCA

I have never done you harm ... So how   Che v'ho fatto in vita mia? ... Son io
can you
inflict all this torture   che cosi torturate! ... Torturate
on my spirit?   l'anima ...
(She bursts into convulsive sobs, mumuring:)
Yes, my spirit, why do you torture my   Si, l'anima mi torturate!
spirit?

(Spoletta continues to pray: 'Nil inultum remanebit!' Taking advantage of Tosca's breakdown, Scarpia crosses to the torture chamber and orders the torture to begin again – a horrible cry is heard – Tosca jumps up and immediately, in a choking voice, rapidly tells Scarpia:)

The well ... in the garden ...   Nel pozzo ... nel giardino ...

SCARPIA

We'll find Angelotti?   Là è l'Angelotti?

TOSCA

Yes!   Si ...
SCARPIA
(loudly, towards the torture chamber)

Stop now, Roberti.   Basta, Roberti.

SCIARRONE
(who has opened the door)

He has fainted.   È svenuto!

TOSCA
(to Scarpia)

You assassin!   Assassino! ...
I want to see him ...   Voglio vederlo ...

SCARPIA

Go, bring him in here!   Portatelo qui!

(Sciarrone returns and then Cavaradossi appears, unconscious, carried by two agents, [23, 24] who lay him on the sofa. Tosca runs to him, but the shock of her lover's face covered with blood is so strong that she covers her eyes in horror – then, ashamed at such weakness, she kneels beside him, kissing him and weeping. – Sciarrone, the Judge, Roberti, and the Secretary go out at the back, while, at a sign from Scarpia, Spoletta and the agents remain.)

CAVARADOSSI
(recovering)

Floria!   Floria! ...

TOSCA
(covering him with kisses)

My darling ...   [15]   Amore ...

CAVARADOSSI

My love ...   Sei tu? ...

TOSCA

How you have suffered,   Quanto hai penato
my dearest love! But God   anima mia! Ma il sozzo
will punish this cruel fiend!   birro la pagherà!

CAVARADOSSI

Tosca, did you tell them?   Tosca, hai parlato?

TOSCA

No, my love ...   No, amor ...

CAVARADOSSI

You promise?   Davver? ...

SCARPIA
(*loudly, to Spoletta*)

The well   [1]   Nel pozzo
in the garden. Go, Spoletta!   del giardin. – Va, Spoletta.

(*Exit Spoletta: Cavaradossi has heard and rises threateningly towards Tosca, but his strength fails him and he falls back on the sofa, bitterly, reproachfully exclaiming to Tosca:*)

CAVARADOSSI

You've betrayed me! ...   Ah! m'hai tradito! ...

TOSCA
(*entreating*)

Mario!   Mario!

CAVARADOSSI
(*pushing Tosca away as she clings tightly to him*)

I reject you!   Maledetta!

(*Sciarrone suddenly bursts in, breathlessly.*)

SCIARRONE

Oh, such fearful news, your lordship!   Eccellenza ... quali nuove! ...

SCARPIA
(*surprised*)

Why this air of anxious hurry?   Che vuol dir quell'aria afflitta?

SCIARRONE

All our armies are defeated ...   Un messaggio di sconfitta ...

SCARPIA

All our troops are defeated? Where?   Che sconfitta? Come? Dove?

SCIARRONE

At Marengo ...   A Marengo ...

SCARPIA
(*impatiently*)

Yes, go on, man!   Tartaruga!

SCIARRONE

Bonaparte has won the day.   Bonaparte è vincitor ...

SCARPIA

Melas?   Melas?

SCIARRONE

No! Melas was beaten!   No. Melas è in fuga! ...

(*Cavaradossi, who has been listening to Sciarrone with mounting agitation, now in his excitement finds the strength to stand up and confront Scarpia menacingly.*)

CAVARADOSSI

Victorious! Victorious!   Vittoria! Vittoria!

63

God of vengeance appear,	[27]	L'alba vindice appar
fill the wicked with fear!		che fa gli empi tremar!
Surge up Liberty,		Libertà sorge,
crushing all tyranny!		crollan tirannidi!

TOSCA

| Mario, quiet be calm, I beg you! | Mario, taci, pietà di me! |

CAVARADOSSI

Do you see me take pride	Del sofferto martir
in the torture you tried ...	me vedrai qui gioir ...
while your blood runs cold,	il tuo cuor trema,
oh Scarpia, you murderer!	o Scarpia carnefice!

(*Tosca desperately embraces Cavaradossi, trying to interrupt him and silence him, while Scarpia replies to him with a sarcastic smile.*)

SCARPIA

Your bluster, shouting, can only	Braveggia, urla! – T'affretta
reveal the depths of infamy	a palesarmi il fondo
in your nature.	dell'alma ria!
You're dead already,	Va! – Moribondo,
for the hangman's noose awaits you!	il capestro t'aspetta!

(*enraged by Cavaradossi's words, he shouts to his agents:*)

| I want him out of here! | Portatemelo via! |

(*Sciarrone and the agents seize Cavaradossi and drag him towards the door – Tosca makes a desperate attempt to embrace him, but to no avail: she is brutally pushed away.*)

TOSCA

| Mario ... with you ... | Mario ... con te ... |

(*The agents lead Cavaradossi away; Sciarrone follows them; Tosca is about to go after them, but Scarpia stands in the way, closes the door, and thrusts her back.*) [26]

SCARPIA

| Not you! | Voi no! |

Tosca – Scarpia

TOSCA
(*with a groan*)

| Oh, save his life! | Salvatelo! |

SCARPIA

| I? ... You! | Io? ... Voi! |

(*He approaches the table, notices his half-finished dinner, and once more becomes calm and affable.*) [20]

| My supper here was sadly interrupted. | La povera mia cena fu interrotta. |

(*seeing Tosca dejected and motionless, still by the door*)

Why so dejected? ... Come, my lovely	Così accasciata? ... Via, mia bella signora
young lady,	
come and sit down. Together we may find	sedete qui. – Volete che cerchiamo
a way of rescuing your lover.	insieme, Tosca, il modo di salvarlo?

(*Tosca starts and looks at him; still smiling, Scarpia sits down, at the same time motioning her to sit too.*)

Now then ... be seated ... and we'll	E allor sedete ... e favelliamo ... E intanto
consider.	
A glass of wine first, a wine from Spain ...	un sorso. È vin di Spagna ...

(*He fills the glass and offers it to Tosca.*)

| A half-glass, | Un sorso |
| it would revive you. | per rincorarvi. |

TOSCA

(*Gazing straight at Scarpia, she slowly approaches the table, sits down resolutely facing him, and asks in a tone of utter contempt:*)

| How much ? ... | Quanto? |

64

SCARPIA
(imperturbably, filling his glass)

How much? . . .   Quanto? . . .

TOSCA

Your price! . . .   Il prezzo! . . .
(He laughs.)

SCARPIA

Ah . . . you offer a bribe; but a lovely [28] Già. – Mi dicon venal, ma a donna bella
woman
must not tempt me with common bribes of   io non mi vendo a prezzo di moneta.
money.
When I betray my oath   [29] Se la giurata fede
of office and trust, I'll ask some other   debbo tradir, ne voglio altra mercede,
payment:
I'll ask a far sweeter payment.   ne voglio altra mercede.
The moment I have prayed for! . . .   Quest'ora io l'attendeva! . . .
How I have ached   [30] Già mi struggea
with love for the diva!   l'amor della diva! . . .
But tonight my eyes were opened: Ma poc'anzi ti mirai
I saw you as a woman!   qual non ti vidi mai!
All your tears were like lava,   Quel tuo pianto era lava
burning my senses,   ai sensi miei
and the hatred darting out of your dark   e il tuo sguardo, che odio in me dardeggiava,
eyes
increased my hungry craving!   mie brame inferociva! . . .
When you sprang like a leopard   Agil qual leopardo
and enfolded your lover,   ti avvighiasti all'amante –
Ah! I vowed that you   in quell'istante
would soon belong to me!   t'ho giurata mia! . . .
Me! Tosca mine!   [29] mia! Sì, t'avrò! . . .
*(He rises, stretching his arms out to Tosca: she has listened motionless, as if turned to stone, to
Scarpia's avowal of lust; now she leaps up and takes refuge behind the sofa.)*

TOSCA
(running to the window)

Ah! Ah! I'll jump out of this window!   Ah! Ah! Piuttosto giù mi avvento!

SCARPIA
(coldly)

Your Mario   In pegno
still remains my prisoner.   il tuo Mario mi resta!

TOSCA

Ah, I despise and hate . . .   Ah! miserabile . . .
(She has a sudden idea to appeal to the Queen and she runs to the door.)
. . . this horrible bargain: L'orribile mercato! . . .

SCARPIA
(ironically)

I won't restrain you by force. You're free to Non ti trattengo. – Libera sei. – Va pure.
go, I mean it.
But your hope is a vain one,   Ma è fallace speranza: la Regina
for the Queen cannot save your lover from   farebbe grazia ad un cadavere!
the hangman's noose.

*(Tosca retreats, stunned with horror, and drops onto the sofa, never taking her eyes off
Scarpia; then she turns her gaze from him in a gesture of supreme disgust and loathing.)*

You detest me!   Come tu m'odii!

TOSCA

Dear God!   Ah! Dio! . . .

SCARPIA
(approaching close to her)

And that is how I want you!   Così, così ti voglio!

Do not touch me, you viper! I hate you, I hate you,   Non toccarmi – demonio – t'odio, t'odio,
despise you, loathe you!   abbietto, vile!

(*She flees in revulsion from Scarpia.*)

SCARPIA

No, not really!   Che importa?
Throbbing with anger ... throbbing with desire!   Spasimi d'ira e spasimi d'amore!

TOSCA

Viper!   Vile!!

SCARPIA

Tosca!   Mia!!

(*He clutches at her.*)

TOSCA

Viper!   Vile!

(*She retreats behind the table.*)

SCARPIA
(*pursuing her*)

Tosca!   Mia ...

TOSCA

Ah, help me! Ah, help me! [26]   Aiuto! – aiuto!

(*A distant roll of drums draws gradually nearer, then fades in the distance.*) [31]

SCARPIA
(*stopping in his tracks*)

Listen!   Odi?
There's the drum beat. They're starting. They will escort   È il tamburo. S'avvia. Guida la scorta
the ones who die tomorrow. And time is passing!   ultima ai condannati. Il tempo passa!

(*Tosca listens in terrible dread, and then comes away from the window, to lean exhausted on the sofa.*)

See! Work is going forward down there already.   Sai quale oscura opra laggiù si compia?
Listen! The gallows for Mario! For your Mario,   Là si drizza un patibolo. Al tuo Mario,
one hour is left – and you have the power to save him.   per tuo voler, non resta che un'ora di vita.

(*He leans callously on the corner of the table, still looking at Tosca.*)

TOSCA
(*in agony*)

Life has taught me singing and loving.	[32] Vissi d'arte, vissi d'amore
I never did harm to one living creature.	non feci mai male ad anima viva!
Often in secret	Con man furtiva
I offered help to the poor and the needy.	quante miserie conobbi, aiutai ...
Daily I pray sincerely.	[13] Sempre con fè sincera
My prayers ascend	la mia preghiera
from so many holy churches in Rome ...	ai santi tabernacoli sali ...
And every day my flowers	Sempre con fè sincera
grace the altar of God.	diedi fiori agli altar.
But now when I am suffering,	Nell'ora del dolore
do you, dear God, reject me?	perchè, perchè, Signore,
Ah, why do you reward your servant so?	perchè me ne rimuneri cosi?
I gave my jewels	[13] Diedi gioielli
for the Madonna's mantle;	della Madonna al manto,
I gave my singing	e diedi il canto

to glorify the angels of Heaven –	agli astri, al ciel, che ne ridean più belli.
yet now in my distress, ah why,	[26] Nell'ora del dolor perchè,
ah why, dear Lord,	perchè, Signor,
ah why, do you reward your servant so?	perchè me ne rimuneri così?

SCARPIA

Your answer!	Risolvi!

TOSCA
(kneeling before Scarpia)

On my knees must I implore you?	Mi vuoi supplice ai tuoi piedi?
Mercy ...	Vedi,
See I stretch out my hands to beg you!	le man giunte io stendo a te!
Hear me! Mercy!	Ecco, vedi,
All I ask is a single	e mercè d'un tuo detto
word of pity ...	vinta aspetto ...

SCARPIA

Such grace and glowing beauty; that [28, 29]	Sei troppo bella, Tosca, e troppo amante.
warm, loving nature;	
I yield. I ask but a trifle.	Cedo. – A misero prezzo
I yield a life up, favour me with one brief	tu, a me una vita, io, a te chieggo un istante!
moment!	

TOSCA
(rising, with a sense of total contempt)

No, no! How you disgust me!	Va – va – mi fai ribrezzo!

(a knock at the door)

SCARPIA

Come in.	Chi è là?

SPOLETTA
(bursting in)

Your Excellency, Angelotti took his life	Eccellenza, l'Angelotti al nostro
on our arrival.	giungere si uccise.

[2]

SCARPIA

So then, let them hang	Ebbene, lo si appenda
his corpse on the gallows. How fares our	morto alle forche. E l'altro prigioniero?
other catch?	

SPOLETTA

The Cavalier Cavaradossi? Everything's	Il cavalier Cavaradossi? È tutto
ready, your lordship.	pronto, Eccellenza.

TOSCA

(Heaven help me!)	(Dio! m'assisti! ...)

SCARPIA
(to Spoletta)

Don't go yet.	Aspetta.

(to Tosca)

Your answer?	Ebbene?

(Tosca nods affirmatively and hides her face, weeping with shame.)

(to Spoletta)

Listen ...	Odi ...

TOSCA
(suddenly interrupting Scarpia)

But give the word to free him	Ma libero all'istante
this instant!	lo voglio ...

SCARPIA
(*to Tosca*)

We have to move with care. I can't
be seen to release him. The world must
believe
that Cavaradossi has been shot.

Occorre simular. Non posso
far grazia aperta. Bisogna che tutti
abbian per morto il cavalier.

(*He points to Spoletta.*)

This faithful man
will arrange it all.

Quest'uomo
fido provvederà.

TOSCA

How may I trust you?　　　　Chi mi assicura?

SCARPIA

I'll give him his orders here in your presence.　　L'ordin ch'io gli darò voi qui presente.
(*to Spoletta*)
Spoletta: close it.　　　　Spoletta: chiudi.

(*Spoletta closes the door, then returns to Scarpia.*)

I have changed my decision.
The prisoner now is to be shot.

Ho mutato d'avviso.
Il prigionier sia fucilato . . .

(*Tosca gives a start of terror.*)

Now mark me –　　　　Attendi . . .
(*He fixes Spoletta with a hard, significant look and Spoletta nods repeatedly to indicate that
he understands what Scarpia means.*)
just as we did in the case of Palmieri . . .　　Come facemmo del conte Palmieri.

SPOLETTA

An execution . . .　　　　Un'uccisione . . .

SCARPIA
(*at once, pointedly*)

. . . in appearance, as we did
with Count Palmieri! You understand me?

. . . simulata! . . . Come
avvenne del Palmieri! . . . Hai ben compreso?

SPOLETTA

I understand you.　　　　Ho ben compreso.

SCARPIA

Go.　　　　Va.

TOSCA

I want permission
to tell him.

Voglio avvertirlo
io stessa.

SCARPIA

You shall.　　　　E sia.
(*to Spoletta*)
You will arrange it. Mind now:　　Le darai passo. Bada:
as dawn is breaking.　　all'ora quarta.

SPOLETTA

Yes. Just like Palmieri . . .　　Sì. Come Palmieri.

(*Exit Spoletta.* [1] *Scarpia stands by the door, listening to Spoletta's retreating footsteps. His
face and whole manner then change, and he advances towards Tosca flushed with passion.*)

SCARPIA

I've done as you commanded . . .　　Io tenni la promessa . . .

TOSCA
(*stopping him*)

Just one moment.
You must give me a safe-conduct so that I
can leave
the country with Mario.

Non ancora.
Voglio un salvacondotto onde fuggire
dallo Stato con lui.

68

SCARPIA
(politely)

You're really set on leaving?   Partir volete?

TOSCA

Yes, for ever!   Si, per sempre!

SCARPIA

I'm always at your service.   Si adempia il voler vostro.
(He crosses to the desk and starts to write, breaking off to ask Tosca:)
Which road have you chosen?   Qual via scegliete?

(As Scarpia writes, Tosca approaches the table [33] and, with a trembling hand, takes the glass of Spanish wine which Scarpia had poured; however, as she raises the glass to her lips she notices a sharp, pointed knife on the table; she glances rapidly at Scarpia, who is absorbed in what he is writing – and with extreme caution gropes for the knife, answering his questions and watching him closely all the time.)

TOSCA

The shortest!   La più breve!

SCARPIA

Civitavecchia?   Civitavecchia?
(writing)

TOSCA

Yes.   Si.

(All the while watching Scarpia, she at last manages to grasp the knife, and hides it behind her while she leans on the table. He completes the safe-conduct, seals it, and folds it up: then with open arms he advances towards Tosca.)

SCARPIA

Tosca, now at last you're mine!   [29] Tosca, finalmente mia! . . .

(But his wanton exclamation changes to a terrible cry – Tosca has stabbed him in the breast.)

Cursed viper!!   Maledetta!!

TOSCA

That was the kiss of Tosca!   Questo è il bacio di Tosca!

(Scarpia stretches an arm out to Tosca, staggering towards her, appealing for help. Tosca retreats from him – but suddenly finds she is caught between him and the table. Realising that he is about to touch her, she pushes him from her in horror. Scarpia falls, howling, his voice half choked with blood.)

SCARPIA

Ah, help me! I'm dying! Ah, help me! I'm dying!	Aiuto! Muoio! Soccorso! Muoio!
Oh! Help me! Oh! Help me! Murder! Please help me!	Soccorso! Aiuto! Muoio! Aiuto!

TOSCA
(watching Scarpia with hatred, as he struggles helplessly, clutching at the sofa, and trying to get to his feet)

Your blood foams and chokes you! Ah!	Ti soffoca il sangue? Ah!
The blow struck by a woman! . . .	E ucciso da una donna! . . .
I repaid all your torture!	— M'hai assai torturata?!

SCARPIA

Please help me! Murder!   Soccorso! Muoio!

TOSCA

Can you still hear me? Tell me!   Odi tu ancora? Parla! . . .

(Scarpia makes a last effort and falls back.)

Look at me! I am Tosca!	Guardami! Son Tosca!
Oh Scarpia!	O Scarpia!!

	SCARPIA
Oh help me, I'm dying!	Soccorso, aiuto!

	TOSCA
Does your blood choke you?	Ti soffoca il sangue?

	SCARPIA
Murder!	Muoio!

	TOSCA
Die and be damned for ever!	Muori dannato! Muori!
Die! Die!	[1] Muori!! muori!!!

	SCARPIA
Ah! . . .	Ah! . . .

TOSCA
(seeing him motionless)

It's over! Now I forgive him!	È morto! . . . Or gli perdono!
This is the man who terrorised Rome like Nero!	E avanti a lui tremava tutta Roma!

(Without taking her eyes off the body, Tosca goes to the table, puts the knife down, dips a napkin in the water jug, and washes her fingers [33]: then she goes to the mirror and arranges her hair. She then looks for the safe-conduct on the writing-desk: not finding it there, she turns and sees that it is in the dead man's clenched hand: with a shudder she extracts it, and conceals it in her bosom. She extinguishes the candles on the table, and is about to leave when a scruple detains her. Seeing that one of the candles on the desk is still alight, she returns and picks it up, lights the other, and places them on either side of Scarpia's head [29]. She rises, looks about again, sees a crucifix, takes it down from the wall, carries it reverently back, kneels, and places it on Scarpia's breast – then she rises, and goes out cautiously, closing the door behind her.)

(Quick curtain.)

Renata Tebaldi as Tosca (Stuart-Liff Collection)

70

Act Three

The platform of Castel Sant'Angelo

On the left, a casemate, furnished with a table (on which stand a lamp, a thick register, and writing materials), a bench, and a chair. A crucifix hangs on one wall, with a lamp suspended in front of it. On the right, the opening to a little staircase leading up to the platform. In the background, the Vatican and St Peter's. [39, 34, 1] *It is still night: this gives way slowly to the uncertain grey twilight that precedes dawn: church bells ring for Matins. A shepherd boy is heard singing as he leads his flock.*

A SHEPHERD BOY

No word can cheer me,	[35, 34]	Io de' sospiri,
My heart is sad and heavy.		Te ne rimanno tanti.
Blow winds and carry		Pe' quante foje
My sighs of love away.		Ne smoveno li venti.
Can you not see		Tu mme disprezzi.
My heart is breaking?		Io mi ciaccoro,
Golden haired beauty,		Lampena d'oro,
Soon I must die!		Me fai morir!

(A gaoler with a lantern comes up from the stairs, goes to the casemate, and lights first the lamp in front of the crucifix, then that on the table: he sits down and waits, half asleep. Then a picket, under a sergeant of the guard, mounts onto the platform, escorting Cavaradossi [36]: they halt, and the sergeant leads Cavaradossi into the casemate, where he hands a document to the gaoler. The gaoler examines this document, opens the register, and writes as he puts his questions.)

Gaoler – Cavaradossi – Sergeant – Soldiers

GAOLER

Mario Cavaradossi? | Mario Cavaradossi?

(Cavaradossi nods. The gaoler hands the pen to the sergeant.)

Please sign. | A voi.

(The sergeant signs the register, then leaves with the soldiers, down the stairs.)

(to Cavaradossi)

One hour is left you.	Vi resta
A priest is here. Will you make	un'ora. Un sacerdote i vostri cenni
your last confession?	attende.

CAVARADOSSI

No. But grant me, I beg you,	No. Ma un'ultima grazia io
one final favour.	vi richiedo.

GAOLER

I'd like to ... | Se posso ...

CAVARADOSSI

I leave behind me	Io lascio al mondo
someone I hold most dearly. Would you	una persona cara. Consentite
give me leave to write her a letter?	ch'io le scriva un sol motto.

(taking a ring from his finger)

All I can offer	Unico resto
to tempt your kindness is this	di mia richezza è questo
gold ring. If you will promise	anel ... Se promettete
that you'll deliver what I write	di consegnarle il mio
to a lady,	ultimo addio,
you may keep it.	esso è vostro ...

(He hesitates for a moment, then accepts and, motioning Cavaradossi to sit at the table, goes and seats himself on the bench.)

I promise. Scrivete.

CAVARADOSSI
(He starts to write [7] . . . but after only a few lines is overcome by memories.) [36]

All the stars shone in heaven and the night air	E lucevan le stelle ed olezzava
was scented. I heard the gate	la terra – e stridea l'uscio
creak open, and then on the pathway a footstep.	dell'orto – e un passo sfiorava la rena.
I breathed her fragrant perfume,	Entrava ella, fragrante,
then she ran to embrace me . . .	mi cadea fra le braccia . . .
Oh sweetest kisses, languishing caresses,	Oh! dolci baci, o languide carezze,
with trembling fingers	mentr'io fremente
I loosed the veil that hid her dark-eyed beauty!	le belle forme disciogliea dai veli!
My dream of love has vanished now for ever.	Svani per sempre il bel sogno d'amore . . .
That hour has faded,	L'ora è fuggita
and now no hope is left me! . . .	e muoio disperato! . . .
And just when life was full of hope and promise!	E non ho amato mai tanto la vita!

(He breaks down sobbing. Up the stairs come Spoletta and the sergeant, followed by Tosca [7]: the sergeant is carrying a lantern. – Spoletta shows Tosca where Cavaradossi is, then calls the gaoler over to him. He, the sergeant, and the gaoler then go back down again, though first instructing a sentry, standing in the background, to keep an eye on the prisoner.)

Tosca – Cavaradossi

(Tosca sees Cavaradossi weeping, his head in his hands. She goes to him and raises his head with both hands. Cavaradossi leaps to his feet in astonishment. With a convulsive movement Tosca hands him a paper, but she is far too overcome with emotion to speak.)

CAVARADOSSI
(reading)

Ah! "Safe-conduct for Floria Tosca . . . and for the man who is her companion." Ah! "Franchigia a Floria Tosca . . . e al cavalier che l'accompagna."

TOSCA
(reading with him in a breathless, unsteady voice)

. . . and for the man who is her companion." . . . e al cavalier che l'accompagna."
(to Cavaradossi with a triumphant cry)
You're free to go. Sei libero!

CAVARADOSSI
(He examines the document and reads the signature.)

Scarpia! [1] Scarpia! . . .
Kindness from Scarpia? His first act of true compassion . . . Scarpia che cede? la prima sua grazia è questa . . .

TOSCA

His final one! E l'ultima!
(She takes back the safe-conduct and puts it in her bag.)

CAVARADOSSI

His final one? Che dici? . . .

TOSCA

He demanded my love for your life.	Il tuo sangue o il mio amore
My tears and my pleas were useless.	volea. Fur vani scongiuri e pianti.
I turned, frantic with fear,	Invan, pazza d'orror,
to the Madonna, but she would not hear [13] me.	alla Madonna mi volsi e ai Santi . . .

Then the monster informed me:	L'empio mostro dicea:
Now the gallows	Già nei cieli
raise their hideous arms to heaven!	il patibol le braccia leva!
The drums began their rolling . . . [31]	Rullavano i tamburi . . .
He gloated on my helpless dilemma, [29]	Rideva, l'empio mostro . . . rideva . . .
sharpened his claws to pounce on his prey!	già la sua preda pronto a ghermir!
"You promise?" – Yes – ready to die	"Sei mia?" – Sì. – Alla sua brama
with shame, I promised. And then my eye [33]	mi promisi. Li presso
was caught by a knife blade . . .	luccicava una lama . . .
He wrote the order that set us free,	Ei scrisse il foglio liberator,
came forward to embrace me.	venne all'orrendo amplesso . . .
Deep in his heart I drove the shining blade.	Io quella lama gli piantai nel cor.

CAVARADOSSI

You? With this hand you destroyed him, for my sake,	Tu? . . . di tua man l'uccidesti! – tu pia,
and you so good and kind!	tu benigna – e per me!

TOSCA

Blood from his heart	N'ebbi le mani
was all over my fingers.	tutte lorde di sangue! . . .

CAVARADOSSI
(*taking Tosca's hands lovingly in his own*)

Oh hands of mercy, innocent and loving! [37]	O dolci mani mansuete e pure
Oh hands intended for compassion and goodness!	o mani elette a bell' opre e pietose,
And made to fondle children and gather roses!	a carezzar fanciulli, a coglier rose,
And join in prayer for those in trouble!	a pregar, giunte, per le sventure,
But those hands fashioned by the God of loving	dunque in voi, fatte dall'amor secure,
were chosen by the sacred goddess of justice.	giustizia le sue sacre armi depose?
His death was your deed, oh hands of [33] retribution,	Voi deste morte, o mani vittorïose,
oh hands of mercy, innocent and loving!	o dolci mani mansuete e pure! . . .

TOSCA
(*freeing her hands*)

Listen . . . dawn is approaching. I gathered [38]	Senti . . . l'ora è vicina; io già raccolsi
(*showing the bag*)	
all my money and jewels . . . a carriage is in waiting.	oro e gioielli . . . una vettura è pronta.
But first . . . and now you will laugh . . . first they are going	Ma prima . . . ridi, amor . . . prima sarai
to shoot you; their rifles will have blank cartridges . . .	fucilato – per finta – ad armi scariche. –
just a sham execution. They fire, you fall.	Simulato supplizio. Al colpo . . . cadi.
Then the soldiers will leave us – and then to freedom!	I soldati sen vanno – e noi siam salvi!
Off to Civitavecchia . . . we'll take a boat there . . .	Poscia a Civitavecchia . . . una tartana . . .
put out to sea!	e via pel mar!

CAVARADOSSI

Liberty!   Liberi!

TOSCA

Liberty!   Liberi!

CAVARADOSSI

Put out to sea!   Via pel mar!

TOSCA

No more grief in all the world.	Chi si duole in terra più?
Smell the scent of roses?	Senti effluvi di rose?

See how every living thing	Non ti par che le cose
awaits the sunrise as if it were a lover!	aspettan tutte innamorate il sole? ...

CAVARADOSSI
(with profound tenderness)

I minded death because I had to leave you,	Amaro sol per te m'era il morire,
for you're the soul of everything I live for;	Da te prende la vita ogni splendore,
my deepest hope, my joy and tender longing	all'esser mio la gioia ed il desire
centre on you, for you alone inspire me.	nascon di te, come di fiamma ardore.
The flashing storms and paling skies	Io folgorare i cieli e scolorire
of heaven take form and colour when you are beside me,	vedrò nell'occhio tuo rivelatore,
and all the glorious beauties of nature	e la beltà delle cose più mire
touch my soul when you love and desire me.	avrà sol da te voce e colore.

TOSCA

Oh Love, that knew the way to win your freedom,	Amor che seppe a te vita serbare
you be our guide on land, our pilot at sea!	cie sarà guida in terra, in mar nocchiere
We'll follow where the voice of love is calling.	e vago farà il mondo a riguardare.
We'll be alone, the two of us together,	Finchè congiunti alle celesti sfere
floating away like clouds as sunset is falling ...	dileguerem, siccome alte sul mare
and then we'll find a paradise for ever.	a sol cadente, nuvole leggere!

(They remain silent, deeply moved: then Tosca, recalling the reality of the situation, looks around uneasily.)

What is keeping them?	E non giungono ...

(She turns to Cavaradossi with eager tenderness.)

Mind now! [38]	Bada! ...
You have to fall at the moment	al colpo egli è mestiere
you hear the soldiers firing.	che tu subito cada ...

CAVARADOSSI
(reassuring her)

I'll not fail you.	Non temere
When they fire I will fall down, utterly lifeless.	che cadrò sul momento – e al naturale.

TOSCA
(insisting)

But do be careful, try to fall correctly!	Ma stammi attento – di non farti male!
I know how to do it,	Con scenica scienza
on the stage we all learn it ...	io saprei la movenza ...

CAVARADOSSI
(He interrupts her, pulling her to him.)

Tell me again of our journey together;	Parlami ancor come dianzi parlavi:
your voice is sweeter than the lark at morning!	è così dolce il suon della tua voce!

TOSCA
(with ever greater emotion, giving free rein to her ecstasy)

United in our exile	Uniti ed esultanti
we shall create a world of love around us	diffonderan pel mondo i nostri amori
with a glory of colour.	armonie di colori ...

TOSCA AND CAVARADOSSI
(in supreme exaltation)

With a glory of music by night and day!	Armonie di canti diffonderem!

(with passionate fervour)

World of love, [39]	Trionfal,
shining with promise,	di nuova speme
flaming with passion,	l'anima freme
ever-increasing	in celestial

74

holy fire . . .	crescente ardor.
We feel your glorious joy . . .	In armonico vol
We hear in our hearts	già l'anima va
music of sweet desire!	all'estasi d'amor.

TOSCA

I'll press upon your eyes a thousand kisses and name you in a thousand whispers of love.

Gli occhi ti chiuderò con mille baci e mille ti dirò nomi d'amor.

(Meanwhile a squad of soldiers has come up the stairs: they are commanded by an officer who draws them up in the background: Spoletta, the sergeant, and the gaoler follow. – Spoletta gives the necessary instructions. The sky lightens; dawn breaks: 4 o'clock strikes. The gaoler approaches Cavaradossi, cap in hand, and points to the officer.)

GAOLER

Ready?   L'ora!

CAVARADOSSI

I am ready.   Son pronto.

(The gaoler takes the register of condemned prisoners and leaves by the stairs.)

TOSCA
(to Cavaradossi, in a low voice, concealing her laughter)

(Don't forget, now . . . you hear them firing . . . down!)

(Tieni a mente: al primo colpo, giù . . .)

CAVARADOSSI
(sotto voce, also laughing)

(Down!)   (Giù!)

TOSCA

(Do not stir till you hear me [38] give a signal.)

(Nè rialzarti innanzi ch'io ti chiami.)

CAVARADOSSI

(No, my darling.)   (No, amore!)

TOSCA

(And fall correctly.)   (E cadi bene.)

CAVARADOSSI

(I'll copy Tosca's performance.)   (Come la Tosca in teatro.)

TOSCA

(Be sensible.)   (Non ridere . . .)

CAVARADOSSI
(pulling a long face)

(Like this?)   (Cosi?)

TOSCA

(Like that.)   (Cosi:)

(Cavaradossi follows the officer [40], after first bowing to Tosca, who positions herself on the left of the casemate, though in such a way that she is able to observe the platform. She sees the officer and the sergeant lead Cavaradossi over to the wall facing her: the sergeant offers to blindfold him: he refuses, with a smile. – These gloomy preliminaries exhaust Tosca's patience.)

TOSCA

What a time they are taking!	Com'è lunga l'attesa!
I can't bear this delay! Sunrise already . . .	Perchè indugiano ancor? . . . Già sorge il sole . . .
Now what else will they think of? It isn't serious,	Perchè indugiano ancora? . . . è una commedia,
I know . . . but still this waiting drives me frantic!	lo so . . . ma questa angoscia eterna pare! . . .

75

(The officer and the sergeant draw up the firing-squad, giving the appropriate orders.)

Now then! At last they are ready . . .   Ecco! . . . apprestano l'armi . . . com'è bello
My dear Mario's so handsome!   il mio Mario! . . .
(Seeing the officer about to bring his sabre down, she puts her hands to her ears, so as not to hear the explosion; then she nods to Cavaradossi to fall.)

      There! Fall now!   Là muori!
     (Seeing him on the ground, she sends him a kiss with her hands.)
        Ah, what an artist!   Ecco un artista! . . .

(The sergeant goes up to the crumpled body and inspects it: Spoletta has also gone over; he draws the sergeant away, preventing him from giving the coup de gràce, then covers Cavaradossi with a coat. The officer lines his men up: the sergeant relieves the sentry in the background, and all go off down the stairs, led by Spoletta. Tosca is intensely agitated, watching all that goes on in a panic lest Cavaradossi, out of impatience, move or speak too soon [40]. Then in a stifled voice to Cavaradossi:)

Oh! Mario, do not stir a while!   O Mario, non ti muovere . . .
They're going now. Quiet! They're going   S'avviano . . . taci! vanno . . . scendono.
  down. There they go.
(As soon as they have left the platform, she goes to listen at the entrance to the stairway: breathless with fear, she suddenly thinks the soldiers are returning to the platform rather than going away – turning to Cavaradossi again, she says in a low voice:)
You mustn't move a muscle yet.   Ancora non ti muovere . . .
     (She listens – they have all gone. She runs to Cavaradossi.)
Quickly up, Mario! Mario! Now quickly,   Presto! su, Mario! Andiamo! . . . andiamo! . . .
  let's go! Up, up!   Su!
Mario! Mario!   Mario! Mario!
(She bends down to help Cavaradossi to his feet: suddenly she gives a choked cry of shock and horror, and looks at her hands, with which she has lifted up the coat. She kneels, tears off the coat, then leaps to her feet again, pale and stunned.)
Murdered! Murdered!   Morto! . . . morto! . . .
(Uttering broken words and sobs of grief, she throws herself on Cavaradossi's body, unable to believe what has happened.)
Oh Mario, murdered? You? Like this? So   O Mario . . . morto? tu? cosi? Finire
  noble
and fine. Why have you left your Floria?   cosi? . . . cosi? . . . povera Floria tua!!

(Meanwhile from the courtyard below the parapet and up the small stairway, the confused voices of Spoletta, Sciarrone, and a number of soldiers are heard approaching.)

SCIARRONE
(off-stage)

I tell you someone's stabbed him!   Vi dico, pugnalato!

CONFUSED VOICES

Scarpia? . . .   Scarpia? . . .

SCIARRONE
(off-stage)

    Scarpia.   Scarpia.

SPOLETTA
(off-stage)

Tosca has done it!   La donna è Tosca!

VOICES, CLOSER

   We must catch her!   Che non sfugga!

SPOLETTA
(off-stage, but closer)

     Keep watch   Attenti
at the bottom of the staircase!   là – allo sbocco delle scale . . .
(Spoletta appears from the stairs, while Sciarrone behind him points at Tosca and shouts:)
      She's there!   È lei!

SPOLETTA
(rushing at Tosca)

Ah! Tosca, you will pay   Ah! Tosca, pagherai
most dearly for his life . . .   ben cara la sua vita . . .

(Tosca leaps to her feet and, instead of fleeing from Spoletta, pushes him violently away, answering:)

TOSCA

With my own!   Colla mia!

(Spoletta staggers back with the unexpected force of Tosca's resistance, while she quickly runs across to the parapet, in front of Sciarrone, who is still on the stairs, and hurls herself into space, crying:)

Oh Scarpia, in sight of God! [36]   O Scarpia, avanti a Dio!

(Sciarrone and a few soldiers emerging in confusion from the staircase, rush to the parapet and look down. Spoletta is left dumbfounded and horror-stricken.)

(Quick curtain.)

The design for Act Three by Adolfo Hohenstein for the first production

Discography /*Martin Hoyle* All complete recordings are in stereo unless asterisked (*) and in Italian. The enthusiast is also referred to *Opera on Record* (ed. Alan Blyth, Hutchinson 1979) for studies comparative and comprehensive of the huge number of excerpts recorded. The present discography includes only recordings currently available in the UK or USA.

Conductor	De Sabata	Molinari-Pradelli	Karajan	Prêtre	Karajan	Levine
Company /Orchestra	La Scala, Milan	Sta Cecilia	Vienna Opera	Paris Opéra	Berlin Opera Chorus	Ambrosian Opera Chorus, Philharmonia
Tosca	Callas	Tebaldi	L. Price	Callas	Ricciarelli	Scotto
Cavaradossi	Di Stefano	Del Monaco	Di Stefano	Bergonzi	Carreras	Domingo
Scarpia	Gobbi	London	Taddei	Gobbi	Raimondi	Bruson
Disc UK number	SLS825	GOS612-3	5BB123-4	SLS917	2707 121	SLS5213
Tape UK number	TC-SLS825		K59K22		3370033	TC-SLS5213
Excerpts (disc)			ASD2300			
Excerpts (tape)				TC2-MOM112		
Disc US number	Angel 3508BL	LON 120	LON 1284	S3655	2707 121	DSX3919
Tape US number		5-1210	5-1284		3370 033	
Excerpts (disc) US				S32326		
Excerpts (tape) US				S32326		

Conductor Company /Orchestra	*Maazel* Sta Cecilia	*Mehta* J. Alldis Choir, New Phil.	*Davis* Royal Opera	*Rescigno* London Opera Chorus, NPO	*Leinsdorf* Rome Opera	*Rostropovich* French National Orchestra
Tosca	Nilsson	Caballé	Freni		Milanov	Vishnevskaya
Cavaradossi	Corelli	Domingo	Carreras	Pavarotti	Björling	Bonisolli
Scarpia	Fischer-Dieskau	Milnes	Wixell	Milnes	Warren	Manuguerra
Disc UK number	SET 341-2	ARL20105	6700 108	D134D2		
Tape UK number			6700 108	K134K22		
Excerpts (disc)	SET 451		6570 158			
Excerpts (tape)	KCET451		7310 158			
Disc US number		ARL20105	6700 108	D12113	VICS-6000	270787
Tape US number		ARK20105	7699 034		V8S-1022	3370008
Excerpts (disc) US		ARL10567				
Excerpts (tape) US						

Bibliography

Mosco Carner has written *Puccini: A Critical Biography* (Duckworth, 1974) which combines rare psychological insight with musical scholarship. It is laid out in three parts (*The Man, The Artist, The Work*) to give a masterly and a very readable survey of every aspect of the subject. Edward Greenfield has written *Puccini: Keeper of the Seal* (London, 1958), and there are a number of beautifully illustrated but less scholarly studies.

Sardou's works are not translated into English, although comparative scenes of *Tosca* are included in Carner's biography. Joseph Kerman's controversial classic *Opera as Drama* was published in 1956 and reissued by Vintage Books in 1972.

Stuart Woolf is the author of a *History of Italy 1700-1860, The Social Constraints of Political Change* (Methuen, 1979) which may be recommended to those who want to know more about the historical background. Harold Acton's *The Bourbons of Naples* (Methuen, 1956, 1974) contains a quantity of lively original source material and an invigorating historical perspective which captures the excitement of the period.

Contributors

Bernard Williams, formerly Knightbridge Professor of Philosophy at the University of Cambridge, is Provost of King's College, Cambridge.

Bernard Keeffe is a conductor and broadcaster, and has devised television programme studies of 'Verdi and The Voice' and 'Puccini The Craftsman'.

Stuart Woolf is Professor of History at the University of Essex.

Edmund Tracey is Director of Drama and Text for English National Opera and has translated numerous operas.